DISCOVER AMERICA

AMERICA

and

FRIENDS SHARING
◆ AMERICA ◆

The Early Travelers by Dawn E. Amos, Rapid City, South Dakota. 1990. Cotton muslin. *First Place Grand Prize Winner*. This dramatic quilt captures an important facet of history, although as the artist cautions, the design should not be taken as a literal statement about who was here first, but rather as her personal interpretation of the contest theme. "There has been a lot of past misunderstanding between Indians and whites," she says, "but in South Dakota this is a year of reconciliation between the two groups, and I wanted a design that would reflect this new understanding." However, she adds, "I hope that people see a lot of different things in the quilt, not only what I say about it." Dawn Amos has based many of her quilt designs on Native American images because she wants her three sons to be proud of their heritage (her husband is half Sioux), but she does not want them to grow up dwelling only on the past—the choice for the future is theirs. The artist draws her inspiration for her designs from a variety of sources—paintings, photographs, art magazines, and many different artists, as well as from her own environment. She works from ideas rather than a completed sketch, and often will make the components of a quilt and then rearrange them until the right combination and balance is struck. "As I move things around, it [the quilt] tells me where to go from there," she says. Most of the colors used in this quilt were created through hand-dyeing in order to obtain the warm and compelling earthy tones that so elegantly complement the design. The artist, who has no formal studio and works in the basement of her house, found it necessary to run outside periodically to check the dyed colors in natural light to make sure they were right! The basement has one advantage, she says—there is lots of room for working and for getting some distance from a quilt once it is pinned to the wall, which often helps pinpoint where problems are. Dawn Amos is a member of the Black Hills Quilters Guild and a state winner in both the Memories of Childhood and Great American Liberty Quilt contests. Her stunning work also placed her as Best of Show at the 1990 American Quilters Society Show.

DISCOVER AMERICA

and

FRIENDS SHARING ◆ AMERICA ◆

Quilt Texts by
Jacqueline M. Atkins, Museum Editor

Dutton Studio Books   New York

In association with the
Museum of American Folk Art   New York

DUTTON STUDIO BOOKS

Published by the Penguin Group
Penguin Books USA Inc., 375 Hudson Street,
New York, New York, 10014, U.S.A.

Penguin Books Ltd, 27 Wrights Lane,
London W8 5TZ, England

Penguin Books Australia Ltd, Ringwood,
Victoria, Australia

Penguin Books Canada Ltd, 2801 John Street,
Markham, Ontario, Canada L3R 1B4

Penguin Books (N.Z.) Ltd, 182–190 Wairau Road,
Auckland 10, New Zealand

Penguin Books Ltd, Registered Offices:
Harmondsworth, Middlesex, England

First published by Dutton Studio Books, an imprint of Penguin Books USA Inc.

First printing, May, 1991
10 9 8 7 6 5 4 3 2 1

Library of Congress
Catalog Card Number: 91-70022

Printed and bound by Dai Nippon Printing Co., Ltd., Tokyo, Japan
Book designed by Nancy Danahy

ISBN: 0-525-24991-5 (cloth); ISBN: 0-525-48591-0 (DP)

CONTENTS

In recent years, quilting as an activity has taken on international scope and dimensions. Quilting provides the common thread that joins diverse groups of people together and heralds the arrival of the global village. Although language barriers may often appear to be an obstacle to international communication and understanding, the appeal of quilts and the spectacular results of the artists' endeavors can effectively overcome these barriers and translate into a special language understood by all.

The Great American Quilt Festival 3, a Museum of American Folk Art Event presented by Northern, the Quilted Bathroom Tissue, Fairfield Processing Corporation/Poly-Fil® and Springmaid® Fabrics, a division of Springs Industries, showcased the quilts shown in this book in New York City in May 1991. Working within the theme "Discover America," individual quilt artists—some comparatively new to quilting, and some with many years of experience to their credit—illustrate through a variety of exciting images their view of the United States, its history, its future, and its presence in the world today. "Friends Sharing America" highlights the combined talents of quilt artists working as a group on their own special interpretation of the contest theme and recalls the days when communal quilting, through quilting "bees," provided both social and functional comforts as well as a sense of sharing and belonging—factors that still play a part today in the reason for quilters working together.

As Honorary Chairperson of The Great American Quilt Festival 3, I was delighted to cut the opening-day ribbon and to have the opportunity to welcome people from around the world to this incredible five-day event. It has given me the opportunity to see the special bond that quilters have with one another and the important role that the old and well-respected activity of quilting now plays in our modern world. The sense of pride in a task well done, the importance of tradition, and the hope for a better tomorrow are values that are as important today as they were yesterday. As you view these quilts, you will see all of these values combined with the personal ideas and discoveries of the quiltmakers themselves, and my hope is that these exciting works will lead you to make some discoveries of your own.

Alice S. Pickering

Alice S. Pickering
Wife of the Permanent
Representative of the United
States to the United Nations

Honorary Chairperson
The Great American Quilt Festival 3

FOREWORD

Fairfield Processing Corporation, the leading producer of quilt batting and polyester fiber manufactured under the name POLY-FIL®, has always made it a priority to promote the fine art of quilting in whatever way possible. The Great American Quilt Festival, coordinated by the Museum of American Folk Art, has been a most agreeable vehicle for the accomplishment of this task.

Since its inception in 1986, Fairfield has seen the Festival blossom from an idea to a renowned quilt show that attracts 35,000 attendees biennially. Fairfield is pleased to support, sponsor, and promote various quilt contests for the Great American Quilt Festival. This year the show will feature the winners of three international quilt contests, one of which is the "Discover America" contest sponsored jointly by Fairfield and Springmaid® Fabrics. In addition, to celebrate Festival 3, Fairfield will present the "Diamonds Are a Girl's Best Friend" extravaganza of quilted and patchwork wearable art.

The Museum of American Folk Art and Fairfield Processing Corporation are continually striving to demonstrate their commitment to the quilt world and Fairfield believes that the Great American Quilt Festival is an ideal opportunity to introduce the general public to the beauty, talent, and fine workmanship that is involved in the quilting process. The Great American Quilt Festival is now a hallmark in the world of fine quilting and we at Fairfield are proud to be associated with it.

For the past few years, Springmaid® Fabrics, a division of Springs Industries, Inc. has been enthusiastically involved with the Museum of American Folk Art in several ways. We began with a licensing program with the museum, which enabled us to become cosponsors of the Great American Quilt Festival. Our licensed patterns consisted of quilting motifs such as Double Wedding Ring, School House, and Alphabet Blocks.

The novice quilter can enjoy using Springmaid's new fall cotton collections because the fabric lines are focused around preprinted panels with myriad patterns to coordinate beautifully. Although the lines feature preprinted panels, the more experienced quilter can still achieve fabulous results using the coordinating calico prints.

Springmaid will be proudly displaying the newest addition to their ongoing COUNTRY FANTASIES® line at this season's Quilt Festival. The group is entitled "Fall Festival" and will be on display in conjunction with Fairfield Processing Corporation.

It is exciting for Springmaid to be a part of the Great American Quilt Festival 3 because of the tremendous exposure that we receive for our cottons. Springmaid's involvement and commitment to the Festival not only shows that we believe in quilting, but that we fully support this fast-growing industry.

PREFACE

The Museum of American Folk Art showcased one of its best multiple-quilt exhibitions ever at The Great American Quilt Festival 3, held at Pier 92 in New York City on May 1-5, 1991. The quilts on display turned the Pier into a lively panorama of color and design, with the Hudson River as an unbeatable backdrop. I am sure it was hard for anyone to name a favorite among the incredibly vibrant displays as there was much for the eye to behold and a great deal of diversity in the subject matter.

The "Discover America" exhibition, the cornerstone exhibit of the Festival, was the largest single display of quilts on the Pier. This exhibition of prizewinning quilts set the tone for our "Discover America" celebration and delighted its viewers with its unique and varied interpretation of the theme. The overall theme was continued with the exhibition of prizewinning group quilts, "Friends Sharing America." These magnificent quilts are outstanding proof that many hands make wonderful work. These large-size quilts reflect the special bond that quilters have with one another and the close friendships and working relationships that developed through the achievement of a common goal are clearly felt. Both these groups of very special quilts are illustrated in this book.

Also displayed at the Pier with the "Discover America" and "Friends Sharing America" quilts were the winning entries from the "Young People's America" fabric-drawing contest. With elements of both naïveté and sophistication, these blocks illustrated the charm of a child's perspective on the surrounding world. This exhibition, coupled with the "Dollmakers' Magic" display of quilted dolls, provided some very special treats for young and old alike!

Our "Discover America" celebration got off to an early Fourth-of-July start with an exhibition of antique patriotic quilts, "Stars and Stripes Forever: Patriotic Quilts from the Marilyn and Milton Brechner Collection." Quilts sporting eagles, banners, shields, and, of course, stars and stripes reflect the great patriotic fervor of the times as well as of the makers. This first-time public showing of this important private collection, with its red, white, and blue color scheme, was a splendid addition to our quilt displays.

The social and political concerns of quilters today and yesterday were vividly captured in the exhibition "Quilts of Conscience." This grouping of antique and contemporary quilts demonstrated the intensity felt by the quiltmakers about the political, social, cultural, and environmental concerns reflected in their quilts. From war to the suffragette movement to current environmental issues, there is no question that this interesting and thought-provoking exhibition expanded the awareness of all who saw it.

Many people have the mistaken idea that quilting only takes place over quilting frames in studios someplace in the rural Midwest, but this myth was quickly dispelled with the contemporary quilts showcased in the "Citiquilts" exhibition. This invitational, open only to quilters in the New York City area, showcased the variety and vivacity of the quilting that is occurring within a major urban environment in a number of diverse settings.

Although only a sampling of the quilts from the "America's Flower Garden" contest were on display at the Festival, the complete collection of winning quilts will be exhibited at the Museum of American Folk Art/ Eva and Morris Feld Gallery at Lincoln Square, New York City, from June 20 to September 15, 1991. This incredible array of color and flowers highlights the talents of quilters who see the world through "rose"-colored glasses! During the Festival, the exhibition at the Gallery was "The Quilt Encyclopedia." This A-to-Z look at quilting included traditional and contemporary quilts, quilted clothing, quilting notions, and quilting accessories. All of the major quilting traditions were represented by pieces from both public and private collections. A very comprehensive overview, indeed!

Anecdotal and historical information was provided by Museum staff members as they led special walking tours of all the exhibitions before the Festival and Gallery opened to the public. This "inside" view of the quilt displays was a high point for many of the attendees at this popular event. The Pier was also a veritable marketplace of wonderful temptations for quilters and quilt lovers alike as more than 140 exhibitors offered for sale antique and contemporary quilts, notions, fabrics, books, craft items, and an incredible array of related textiles.

The comprehensive programming for The Great American Quilt Festival 3 was truly a "Discover America" celebration. For the first time, all of the lectures were presented on the Pier at the Festival itself, while workshops, seminars, and evening programs were held off-site at the Festival headquarters hotel. On each of the five days, the lectures at the Festival focused on a particular aspect of quilting—that is, collecting, decorating, historic quilts, and contemporary quiltmaking. The workshops and lectures continued discussion on and enhanced the lecture topics in a smaller forum.

Historical lectures "blanketed" the country by including presentations on Pennsylvania, New York, Virginia, Alabama, Mississippi, Tennessee, North and South Carolina, and California, and on Native American and African-American quilts. Quilts as a means of personal expression was the theme explored as topics ranged from autobiographical close-ups of the work of several well-known contemporary quilters to an exploration of quiltmaking as an expression of social concerns. The theme of inventive quiltmaking included topics focusing on the innovative and embellishment techniques that can transform a good quilt into a great one. The family was the focus for the final day of the Festival and topics were geared to capture the interest of the whole family, along with hands-on workshops for children, and a lecture on quilting from the male perspective.

The wide range of half-day and all-day workshops offered during the five days of the Festival truly provided something for everyone's individual interests and tastes. Subjects included design techniques, color workshops, machine appliqué, and hand-quilting. The traditional as well as the contemporary were highlighted through classes ranging from Crazy quilting to working with mixed media to nature. Rounding out the program were seminars on collecting and caring for both old and new quilts and starting a quilt business.

The festivities continued each evening with the awards ceremony for prizewinning quilts, an international "show and share," and a fashion "show and share" parade. The final evening event was the always-memorable Fairfield Processing Fashion Show, hosted by Donna Wilder. This twelfth-anniversary show, with the theme "Diamonds Are a Girl's Best Friend," was truly a "sparkler"! It was wonderful to end the Festival on such a high note.

The success of this programming series would not have been possible without the incredible teaching staff for The Great American Quilt Festival. It is a great pleasure to be able to make a special acknowledgment of the following artists, craftspeople, and historians who participated: Ellen Ahlgren, Virginia Avery, Cuesta Benberry, Elizabeth Busch, *Country Living Magazine* Staff, Laura Fisher, Fran Fuller, Carter Houck, Janet Page-Kessler, Phyllis Klein, Lee Kogan, Jeannette Lasansky, Jean Ray Laury, Leslie Levison, Emiko Toda Loeb, Terri Mangat, Merrill Mason, Edith Mitchell, Ruth McDowell, Barbara Moll, Anita Murphy, Paula Nadelstern, Margaret Ordonez, Mary Coyne Penders, Bets Ramsey, Heidi Read, Jennifer Regan, Faith Ringgold, Cynthia Elyce Rubin, Susan Shie, Penny Sisto, Fran Soika, Doreen Speckman, Phyllis Tepper, Helene Von Rosenstiel, Elizabeth Warren, Judi Warren, John Willard, Erma Martin Yost, and Shelly Zegart.

And, only through the singular and combined efforts of the following people could such a large and incredible event as The Great American Quilt Festival be produced:

- The "Discover America" contest was made possible through the generous support of its sponsors, Fairfield Processing Corporation/Poly-fil® and Springmaid® Fabrics, a division of Springs Industries.

- USAir graciously provided the air transportation for the grand prizewinners for the "Discover America" contest.

- Our very professional judges for the "Discover America" and "Friends Sharing America" contests were truly a delight. A thank you to them for providing their special brand of expertise.

- All of the interviews for the material included in this book were carried out by Jacqueline Atkins, Sheila Brummel, Jeanne Riger, Edith Garshman, Caroline Hohenrath, and Noriko Fuku. Their outstanding endeavors produced insightful results that let us look for a moment into the lives of these special quiltmakers. The texts for the book were coordinated, written, and edited by Jacqueline Atkins. Through her skillful efforts, she always makes this difficult task look so easy.

- The preparation for the contest judgings was facilitated by the assistance of interns Hui-Ling Hsu and Caroline Kerrigan.

- Through the remarkable efforts of the staffs of the Museum of American Folk Art and Sanford L. Smith and Associates, Ltd., major event producers and managers, The Great American Quilt Festival 3 was truly an outstanding success. Special thanks to Museum staff member Karla Friedlich for her work as Program Chairperson for the Festival.

- The responsibility for the contest and the planning of the many complex elements of the Festival is not a simple job. Our sincere thanks and appreciation to Cathy Rasmussen, Museum staff member, for accomplishing the impossible on our behalf.

Robert Bishop
Director
Museum of American Folk Art

Dare to Dream by Jaime L. Morton, Casa Grande, Arizona. 1990. Cotton, gold lamé, metallic thread. *Second Place Grand Prize Winner.* This quilt, showing Columbus both as a young dreamer and as a mature man on the brink of discovery, has a broader meaning as well. "So many people came to America with dreams for a better way of life," the artist says. "To me, America is a place where people can set their goals high and achieve them. We still have the opportunity to dream—and to succeed." *Dare to Dream* actually is a default design. "My first design showed Columbus looking through a telescope. I had it all drawn out when my husband, an astronomer, told me that telescopes weren't invented until over one hundred years later!" Thus, when Jaime Morton settled on this design, she was careful to research all parts of it for accuracy. Her research also taught her more about Columbus and the knowledge and technology of his time; "It's amazing that he *ever* found land," she notes. The moon and star quilted into the upper corners of the quilt represent the methods of navigation open to mariners of Columbus's day, as well as the fact that the first sighting of America was by moonlight. The quilt, the first designed entirely by the artist, was done on a tight schedule. "I had to set a deadline for finishing each facet of the quilt—Columbus as a boy, as a man, the banner, and so forth. Luckily my kids are old enough to fix their own meals!" The print fabric used in the tunic of the young Columbus set the overall color tone, and overdyeing and bleaching provided the specific shades needed for other parts of the design. The ship was the most difficult part of the quilt to complete. "Originally the design did not include the ship, but it became clear that something was needed for balance," she says. "I did the ship's body three times—I couldn't seem to get the color right." At one point, she even threw the ship pattern in the trash; her husband, however, rescued it, and she finally solved the color problem by using the reverse side of the fabric. Jaime Morton is a member of American Quilters Society, the Arizona Quilt Guild, and the Cactus Quilters.

INTRODUCTION

Choosing a theme for the contest sponsored by the Museum of American Folk Art and held in conjunction with The Great American Quilt Festival is never an easy task. A great deal of thought and consideration are given to the topics selected as we try to chose one with which people can identify, as well as one that lends itself to both contemporary and traditional interpretations and has universal appeal. This can be much more of a challenge than it sounds!

The "Discover America" theme evolved from an open forum on what the Museum's direction would be at the time of the next contest. Although originally conceived around the 500th anniversary of Columbus's arrival in America, the whole premise of "discovery" eventually expanded far beyond that as we realized the potential such a theme could have. It was a topic that instantly appealed to everyone primarily because it broadened the overall scope of the contest beyond simply a recognition of Columbus's voyage and opened up so many diverse possibilities for interpretation. With this in mind, our hope was that people would include images of their own personal discoveries of America. Whether this would be accomplished through special remembrances of a particular vacation spot, exploring life in America through books, television, or films, or reflections on one's ethnic origins, the avenues to travel seemed endless.

Because previous contests had focused on the talents of individual quiltmakers and more limited themes, we decided, as an experiment, to expand "Discover America" to include a series of possibilities. A total of four contests emerged from this central idea: "Discover America"—crib-size quilts made by individuals; "Friends Sharing America"—full-size quilts executed by groups; "Young People's America"—fabric drawings created by children; and "America's Flower Garden"—full-size quilts done by individuals. The quilts illustrated in this book are the winning entries from the "Discover America" and "Friends Sharing America" contests.

For the "Discover America" contest, the crib-quilt size of 45″ x 54″ was chosen, and a two-inch variance in either direction was permissible for entering. This size was selected to facilitate the execution of the theme. Even though we always hope that the entries we receive will be a balance of pictorials and pieced/ geometric pieces, experience has shown that the pictorials win out. With this as a reference, this acceptable "wall-hanging" size lent itself to the expected form of design submissions. Thus, all the winning quilts shown in this book for the "Discover America" contest conform to the 45″ x 54″ format, plus or minus two inches.

Once the size and theme had been decided, the rules for the contest were prepared in time for distribution at The Great American Quilt Festival 2 in April 1989. This allowed quilters attending somewhat of a head start on things as the contest deadline for slide submission was not until September 5, 1990.

The contest was open to quilters worldwide. The entering quilts could be the work of only one person and had to be made from an original design by the entrant. An original use, interpretation, or adaptation of a traditional pattern or patterns was also acceptable.

Quilts also had to conform to the true definition of a quilt, that is, be constructed of a top, batting, and backing. The three layers of the quilt had to be quilted by hand, as no machine quilting or tying was permissible under the rules. Piecing, appliqué, or embroidery could be used in executing the design of the quilt and these techniques could be used separately or in conjunction with one another. Both appliqué and embroidery had to be worked by hand, although piecing could be done on a sewing machine as long as no machine stitching would show on the surface of the quilt.

The "Friends Sharing America" contest was developed to draw on the "Discover America" theme, and the contest was open to groups worldwide. "Group" was defined as three or more people, and all participants had to have worked on the quilt. As with the rules for "Discover America," the quilts had to be an original design or an original interpretation of a traditional pattern by the entrants. Obviously, friendship was the central focus, but we hoped the idea would be expanded into other areas. The feelings of accomplishment in working toward a single goal, the binding threads of friendship, a shared memory of a place or special occasion, and involvement in one's community were all the potential possibilities that could be explored.

The full-size dimensions of 72″ x 72″ were chosen for the "Friends Sharing America" quilts. As with the "Discover America" rules, a two-inch variance in either direction was permissible, and the nine winners included in this section of the book adhere to these dimensions. This size seemed the most natural to select, as it would allow easy group participation. With the full-size quilt, the possibilities for interpretative designs, whether pictorials or more traditional patterns, would have the freedom necessary for development.

With the rules for the "Friends Sharing America" contest also available at the April 1989 Festival, quilters had an early preview on what the group requirements would be as the contest was not over until October 2, 1990. The quilt had to be constructed of a top, batting, and backing. The same three techniques—piecing, appliqué, or embroidery—had to be employed as in the "Discover America" rules; however, for the first time, a sewing machine could be used to execute all three techniques. In addition, the three layers of the quilt could either be done by hand or by machine.

For both contests, upon completion of the quilt, entrants needed to submit four slides along with the entry form. A full shot of the quilt was, obviously, the most important. Three close-up shots were required to show the highlighted areas—the border or binding, the quilting, and the piecing, embroidery, or appliqué. This allowed the judges the best overall viewing of the piece submitted.

Entry forms asked for the title of the quilt as well as a brief description of it. The technique employed on the surface of the quilt also needed to be included. Last, but not least, the entrant was asked to provide any special meaning for the design, stitches, or materials chosen. This very pertinent information was read aloud to the judges during the actual judging processes. The information provided increases the judges' understanding of the design and helps them to comprehend the intended goal of the quilter in making the piece.

At the first stage of judging, which is by slides, the judges are apprised of the criteria to be used to evaluate the quilts. The quilt must conform to the overall theme of the contest, the originality of the design needs to be clearly evident, and the general overall appearance of the work must be pleasing. The craftsmanship and/or needlework are, of course, important aspects, as they can make the difference between a good quilt or a great one. Only the pieces that meet these requirements

were selected by our judges. It should also be noted that all judging is anonymous; judges have no idea who the quiltmakers are nor what their experience is.

The makers of the quilts chosen by the panel of judges for each of the contests were then notified to send the actual quilts for the next and final stage of judging. This second judging is always the harder one as the quilts usually have more impact than the slides and the final decisions become that much more difficult. It is also more apparent to the judges how hard every entrant has worked and how much time and effort have gone into their creations. Much deliberation goes on at these final sessions, as every effort is made to be as fair as possible and each piece is allowed ample time for review. This is never an easy task, as the panels of judges for both contests were well aware of how much of the quilters themselves were represented in their quilts. The quilts illustrated in this book are the final outcome of this intense judging process, and all embody the requirements that constitute a "winning" quilt.

In a grand finale of the judging process, the judges selected the two grand prizewinners from each contest. A great deal of thought and review goes into the judges' final decisions for the grand prizes. An "inner circle" of quilts comes into being, as only a very select number of quilts make the grade for consideration for the top honors. Some of these quilts may ultimately receive special recognition or judge's choice awards if they do not receive grand prizes. Prizes for the "Discover America" and "Friends Sharing America" contests were $5,000 each for first place and $2,500 each for second place.

The distinguished panels of judges clearly rose to the occasion and met the challenge wholeheartedly, as can be seen by the results. Their professionalism, candor, and good humor provided insight and understanding as well as facilitating the whole judging procedure.

The judges for "Discover America" were: Patti Bachelder, Editor of *Quilting Today*; Tracey Inskeep, Springs Industries; Elizabeth V. Warren, Curator of the Museum of American Folk Art; and Donna Wilder, Director of Marketing, Fairfield Processing Corporation.

The judges for "Friends Sharing America" were: Beth Bergin, Membership Director of the Museum of American Folk Art and Editor of the *Quilt Connection*; Paula Nadelstern, author of *Quilting Together* and two-time New York State winner in the Museum's two previous contests; and Cyril I. Nelson, a senior editor at Penguin USA and compiler of *The Quilt Engagement Calendar*.

The "Discover America" and "Friends Sharing America" quilts are exhibited for the first time at The Great American Quilt Festival 3, May 1-5, 1991, here in New York City. After this initial viewing, the quilts will be part of a touring exhibition for three years. Upon completion of the tour, the quilts, with the exception of the grand prizewinners, which become part of the permanent collection of the Museum of American Folk Art, will be returned to their owners.

Conforming the design of a quilt to the theme of a contest is always a challenge for the quiltmaker. This seems even more so in the case of the contests sponsored by the Museum of American Folk Art, as the themes are usually more specific than in many other contests. To enter requires talent, ingenuity, artistic flair, a great sense of color and design, and skill with a needle. These necessities, coupled with a great deal of time spent executing the piece, add up to an incredible commitment to the project. Certainly, contest competitions are not for the faint of heart!

All of this effort and energy is clearly evident to me as I personally catalog each slide and record each of the entry form statements. Knowing the significance of the colors chosen or how the maker hand-dyed each of the fabrics for just the right shading all help bring the quilts—and their makers—to life. The first-time contest entrant writing about her excitement over her design or the seasoned veteran thinking this might be her last quilt are equally precious to me. Quilters related their memories of the past that surfaced while working on their piece, along with their hopes for the future both for themselves and for their families. As judgings are done anonymously so that everyone is evaluated equally, only I know which quilts are done by beginners, which are done by men or women, and which are done by experienced contest winners; this anonymity forms a special bond.

The group-quilt entries particularly touched me with their narratives about how this experience of working together had enriched their lives. With each stitch, acquaintances were transformed into friends and lasting memories were made. Now that they had worked effectively together as a group, many said they would continue to do so.

International quilters' perceptions of things American were also revealing, charming, clever, and thought-provoking—and sometimes all at once! Although the quilts from U.S. entrants covered a wide scope, international entrants focused on American icons and ideals. It was a revelation as to how varied the opinons—and conceptions—could be.

After living with the quilts for so long it is difficult for me not to form certain attachments. Admittedly, I do have my favorites by the time the final judging comes around; however, my role in the proceedings is to be an unbiased coordinator and to keep my personal preferences out of the judging process. This does not mean that tears aren't occasionally shed when a particular favorite fails or that a special feeling of satisfaction might not occur when the judges' opinion also matches mine!

In all, serving as Director for the Quilt Festival has been sometimes an overwhelming experience, but always a heart-warming one—and one that leaves me with wonderful memories as well as a great sense of anticipation for the future!

CATHY RASMUSSEN
Director
The Great American Quilt Festival 3
Museum of American Folk Art

DISCOVER
AMERICA

An Indian View of Discovery by Linda Waselkov, Fairhope, Alabama. 1990. Cotton, ultrasuede. This unusual quilt was, says the artist, "inspired by the maps drawn on deerskin by some of the early southeastern Indian tribes. They show the Indian tribes as circles and the European settlements as squares, depicting an Indian perspective of America at the time of the European 'discovery'." Her facsimile map, broadly representing the whole of the continental United States, has been placed in an ocean of blue fabric in which European ships sail to and fro. Linda Waselkov was exposed to the maps as a result of the research her husband, an archaeologist, was carrying out, and she found them fascinating. She recalls being especially intrigued with the use on the maps of a connecting red line, or road, indicating bad blood between certain groups and a white one indicating a peaceful link between them, and she made effective use of the concept in this work. The "beautiful drawings on the maps that I saw and the unique view of life that they expressed" were particularly moving, she notes, and she regrets the fact that so much of these early cultures disappeared so quickly. Although the figures of the Indian and the deer are similar to illustrations found on actual maps, the others that she used are symbolic in nature and are meant to represent different areas of the country. A kachina doll and a whale represent, respectively, the Southwest and the Northwest, while the fleur-de-lis represents France's influence in the New World, the lion rampant England's, and the castle, Spain's. The four pairs of red triangles at the top and bottom of the map represent the hooves of the deer. The quilting design used in the border is also Indian-inspired; it is derived from early shell engravings. The artist used ultrasuede to represent the deerskin of the map and, she notes, it proved particularly difficult to quilt! Linda Waselkov, a self-taught quilter, has made approximately fifteen crib quilts—most of which she has given away, but a few of which found their way to her two young children, aged four and six years old.

Gridlock 1999 by Liz Piatt, Orinda, California. 1990. All cotton. Every driver's nightmare is amusingly reflected in this whimsical quilt of a multilayered California freeway. At the very lowest level, a multitude of posters extoll the beauties of California and all the interesting things there are to discover in the state. "California is such a big and beautiful state," the artist says; "I tried to give an idea of what there is to see, *if* you can get there!" The posters provided the inspiration for this design, and the artist notes that she, at least, has managed to visit almost all the places advertised in the posters on her quilt. Liz Piatt's imaginary gridlocked freeway is crowded with every conceivable vehicle that might be seen on any well-traveled highway in the country, from the smallest to the largest. Even the vacation car, with a bicycle strapped to the roof, is not forgotten. She used cars and trucks that members of her own family have owned as models for many of the vehicles. Other vehicles represent American icons—Coca-Cola, Good Year, L'Eggs, and so on—that we often see on city streets as well as the highways. The artist notes that even though the quilt idea was meant to be humorous, she realized as she worked on it just how crowded this country has become, especially in the urban areas. Still, she had a good time working on this piece. "It just got more exciting," she says. "When there is a contest, I do my best work. I like the challenge and working out the theme." Liz Piatt has been quilting for about ten years and is basically self-taught, although she had learned general sewing skills in high school—"I remember sewing decorations for our high school dances." She likes the look of art forms in cloth, and most of her quilts are pictorial. One of her major projects was a quilt with fifty-two panels representing all the animals to be found in Yosemite National Park; the quilt was exhibited at Yosemite and was a prizewinner at the California State Fair. The artist also does volunteer work, and sometimes she finds herself racing through her housework so she has time for all her activities—especially quilting!

Reflections on a Summer Vacation by Sherri Bain Driver, Englewood, Colorado. 1990. All cotton. A discussion of glasses and contact lenses at a quilting bee led to this artist's choice of format in interpreting the contest theme. The lenses of five pairs of oversized sunglasses with wildly varying frame patterns reflect the diversity of the landscape of this country. (In fact, she so liked the idea of the glasses that she put a pair of red plaid sunglasses—inspired by a pair owned by a friend—on the back of the quilt.) The scenes are ones the artist recalls from a series of summer-vacation road trips that she and her family made and give a sense of her own discovery of the country through these trips. "I wanted to convey all of America, and it is so varied!" she says. These simple scenes contain a variety of small delights—an infinitesimal windmill peeks over the horizon of the Great Plains, a bird is a fleck in the air above the mountains, a lone cactus stands in stately splendor amid the white sands of the desert, a sand castle is lapped by waves created from turned-back and pleated fabric— and carefully stitched into the quilt border are all the vehicles that one is likely to encounter on the highways of America. Sherri Bain Driver enjoys entering contests for two reason—the themes act as a stimulant to creativity, and the deadlines keep up the pressure to get the quilt done. "I need deadlines," she admits with good humor. She has completed about twenty quilts and has twenty unfinished ones in various stages of completion; "I can have ten going at any one time," she says. She tries to quilt at least a few minutes every day, but some days she may work for as long as nine or ten hours. As the wife of a Navy man, the artist found that quilting provided a comfort and an area of stability—particularly in the years when her husband's career required frequent moves. Her father, one of her biggest quilting fans, died while she was making this quilt, and at one point she wondered if she would be able to complete it, but finish it she did. The artist, who taught needlepoint, crewel, and smocking before she began to quilt in earnest six years ago, belongs to the Arapahoe County Quilters.

Foliage Season by Marianne Haeni, Stamford, Connecticut. 1990. All cotton. Fan-shaped splashes of crimson, gold, and rust wash over this quilt in a graduated and potent burst of jewel-like color that fairly shouts New England in the fall. The quilter, a native of Switzerland, was stunned by the vividness of the leaves on her first trip to Vermont to see the fall foliage, and she found the flaming trees a wonderful discovery in themselves. She was so impressed by the sight that she simply had to stop on the way home to buy fabric that would match the vibrancy of the tones shimmering in the nearby woods. The colors of the leaves are caught in the body of the quilt, but their shapes are echoed in the appliquéd forms representing fallen leaves and the undulating leaf quilting in the borders; the delicate fan shapes themselves, containing all the colors of fall, recall leaves gently floating to the ground. In working on this quilt, she found the rounded edges of the fan shapes to be the most difficult to execute, but, she notes, "the beautiful colors of the fabric kept me going." The quilt is done with all cotton fabrics; "now if only I could afford all silks…," the artist sighs. Although Marianne Haeni has made over a dozen quilts, this is the first one that she has entered in a contest. "The theme interested me, especially since I am gradually exploring and discovering different parts of the country on vacations," she says. She also believes that this design evokes a feeling of independence and freedom, which, she notes, characterizes America for her. The artist, trained as a translator, first learned to quilt in the mid-1980s in Switzerland, when she was in search of a new hobby and found herself to be inspired by Amish quilts; she later followed up her interest with workshops in design and color theory and now has a well-rounded perspective on her evolving art. She likes to set aside at least a little time every day for work on her quilting, when her other activities allow her to do so. Marianne Haeni is a member of the Berne Quilters Guild in Switzerland and of the Nutmeg Quilters Guild here.

Long May She Wave by Dory Sandon, Lake Park, Florida. 1990. Cotton, satin. *Judge's Choice*. The model for this striking half-face view representing an American woman with flowing hair composed of the Stars and Stripes was the artist's nine-year-old daughter. "Katherine is so proud that her face is on the quilt that won a prize from the Museum of American Folk Art," says the equally happy mother! The quilt is the third in a series of three that the artist has done with the flag as a theme; the first of which, entitled *American Quilter*, is now in a corporate collection and the second, *Long May She Survive*, is on exhibit at the Boca Museum of Art. The series was Dory Sandon's own interpretation of the debates over the handling of the flag and resulted in a personal rediscovery of what the flag meant to her. "The flag embodies the people and the people embody the flag," she says. "The two need each other; they are one and the same. The flag is so integral and important to the people of the country; it should be respected." The intricately pieced work proved to be frustrating as well as rewarding, particularly in the mechanics of joining the various components. The eye area was especially difficult, she notes, and there were even times "when I wanted to put it all into the garbage can!" The quilt is pieced entirely by machine but quilted by hand, and both hand-dyed and hand-painted fabrics were used to create the overall three-dimensional effect, particularly in the areas around the eye and lips. Dory Sandon, a full-time quilter whose work is well-known in galleries around the country and is included in a number of corporate collections, is a member of the Norton Museum Art Guild, the Palm Beach County Quilters Guild, and the Professional Artists Committee for the Palm Beach County Council of the Arts. Although she had learned to quilt at the age of eight, she began to quilt regularly in the early 1980s—"I wanted to quilt a tablecloth so that I wouldn't have to iron it," she recalls—and she has now made over one hundred quilts. She works almost every day on her quilts for about ten hours because "quilting is now a full-time business for me."

11

Reaching for the Moon in America by Sara Ann McLennand, Wellington, Florida. 1990. Cotton, cotton blends, velvet, chintz, fringe, metallic thread. In an unusual interpretation of the theme, this artist chose an image that, to her, personifies modern-day woman in America. "It seems to me that she can reach for the moon and get it," she says. "I believe that women have come a long way. I know I have." The quilt represents a woman's dreams and her ability to achieve those dreams; "quilting has provided that for me," she adds, especially when she knows that her work is appreciated by others. The idea for the design came to her while playing cards and watching television with some friends. "There was a magic show on," she recalls, "and when I looked up what caught my eye was the set design. A fat lady was standing on a ladder and reaching out for the stars on the backdrop. I knew that this was it." She grabbed a pencil and paper and immediately began to sketch out the scene so she could later elaborate it further for her quilt. "It took a long time to develop the idea for the quilt and to plan it," she notes "I spent two weeks drawing and redrawing it, and a week finding just the right fabrics. After that, everything just fell into place—I didn't have to rip any sections out or do anything over!" Luckily so, she adds, because she had misread the contest deadline and thought she had more time than she actually did. When she realized her mistake, there were many days of twelve-hours-at-a-stretch quilting to make up the time! "My husband is very supportive of my endeavors," she says, especially when there is a deadline. "He thinks nothing of having peanut butter and jelly sandwiches or scrambled eggs for dinner." Sara Ann McLennand is a member of the Palm Beach Quilters Guild, the American Quilters Society, and the National Quilters Association. She is now working on a series of quilts with an architectural theme. She likes to work within the framework of a series because, she finds, it helps her to explore an idea more fully and allows additional opportunities for developing all the possibilities of a certain theme.

Distant Shores by Wendy Analla, Ellabell, Georgia. 1990. All cotton. In developing her quilt design, the artist carefully researched encyclopedias and other books to find an accurate ship and appropriate costumes for her figures, but she decided to indulge in one bit of historical inaccuracy—she placed the New World scene on the right-hand side and the European scene on the left because "it made it a more pleasing composition." She made full-sized drawings of the three parts of the quilt—the people seeing Columbus's small flotilla off from Spain, an Indian in the fastness of the forest watching the arrival of the newcomers, and the centerpiece—the flagship alone on the sea. Then she placed the fabric a piece at a time on the drawings as it was cut out. The three component scenes are tied together by a pieced-and-painted length of rope (she notes that there are six shades of yellow in each segment of rope) that twines in and around the other design elements and ultimately serves as a frame for the ship. The idea of the rope as a frame came from a stained-glass window with a nautical theme that this artist had also designed. She used both dyeing and marbleizing to achieve the subtle color gradations in water and sky, and almost every piece in the quilt has been hand-painted to give a greater sense of perspective and depth. The painting led to some discouraging moments, however; the sky was initially too pale a blue, and when painting the Indian, she smeared the paints and had to remove the figure. "I ended up appliquéing that Indian three times," she recalls. As she carried the quilt around with her, working on it whenever and wherever she could, children were always interested in what she was doing and curious about the contest, quilting, and the theme—"however," she says, "they had no trouble recognizing Columbus and his ship!" Wendy Analla has found inspiration for her work in her grandmother, a skilled lace maker and crocheter. "I think she would have been proud of me," says the artist, a member of the Embroiderers Guild of America and the Arkansas Quilters Guild and a Memories of Childhood state winner.

Discover America One Patch at a Time by Joyce Winterton Stewart, Rexburg, Idaho. 1990. All cotton. *Best Interpretation of Theme in Traditional Style*. Over 175 different fabrics were used to create the fifty blocks—each representing one state—that comprise this quilt. Not only is each block tied to a state (for example, Maine, the Pine Tree State, is represented by a Pine Tree block), the quilt back offers further information, such as the state's nickname, capital, and largest city, state motto, bird, gem, or flower. Thus, says the artist, "By looking at the quilt blocks and then reading the informaiton on the back, the viewer is able to 'Discover America'!" Although many of the blocks are traditional patterns or variations of them, others are original creations (such as the Robin block for Michigan), and some are whimsical (half of the Lady of the Lake block—for Minnesota—has been transformed into a fish swimming in the lake). Joyce Stewart found that the hardest part of this quilt was fitting in all fifty blocks, for forty-eight, or six blocks by eight blocks, would be the logical sequence. The internal border (composed, the quilter says, of leaves because they are common to *all* the states) solved the problem by allowing her to capture twenty blocks within it and arrange thirty around it. The quilt required time-consuming research, both for the block designs and the information about each state, but it provided a "relearning" experience that the artist found particularly enjoyable. Just as the piece was ready to be quilted, however, the quilter's daughter pointed out that three states on the hand-lettered back were out of order, and so another back had to be made. The reward came when everyone who saw the quilt on the frame were curious enough to crawl under it to read the information lettered on the back! Joyce Stewart, a quilter for over eight years, has won many awards for her work, including a Second Place ribbon in the 1989 American Quilters Society Show for the Amateur Wall Hanging category and state winner in the two previous Great American Quilt Festival contests. "After winning those two," she says, "I just had to try again when this contest came around!"

Oklahoma	Pennsylvania	Hawaii	New Mexico	Colorado	West Virginia	Alaska	Delaware
California							South Dakota
Arkansas	Idaho	Maine	Nevada	Wisconsin			Washington
Vermont	Texas	Iowa	Oregon	South Carolina			Mississippi
Connecticut	New Jersey	Kentucky	Louisiana	Alabama			Minnesota
Maryland	Kansas	Virginia	Illinois	New Hampshire			Michigan
New York	North Carolina	Tennessee	Indiana	Rhode Island			Montana
Florida							Ohio
Arizona	Missouri	Utah	Georgia	North Dakota	Nebraska	Wyoming	Massachusetts

Each quilt block in Joyce Winterton Stewart's quilt is named after a state or represents some special attribute or identifying factor about the state. Use this guide to find your state: *Alabama*, Cottons Reels; *Alaska*, Star of the North; *Arizona*, Prickley Pear; *Arkansas*, Arkansas Traveler; *California*, California; *Colorado*, Rocky Mountains; *Connecticut*, Hope of Hartford; *Delaware*, Log Cabin; *Florida*, Key West Beauty; *Georgia*, Peaches; *Hawaii*, Pineapple; *Idaho*, Gem of the Mountains; *Illinois*, Chicago Pavements; *Indiana*, Indiana Puzzle; *Iowa*, Iowa Rose; *Kansas*, Kansas Star; *Kentucky*, Kentucky Chain; *Louisiana*, Magnolia Bud; *Maine*, Pine Tree; *Maryland*, Oak Tree; *Massachusetts*, Lighthouse; *Michigan*, Robin; *Minnesota*, Lady of the Lake; *Mississippi*, Water Wheel; *Missouri*, Trail of the Covered Wagon; *Montana*, Rocky Mountain Puzzle; *Nebraska*, Corn and Beans; *Nevada*, Card Trick; *New Hampshire*, Granite Rock; *New Jersey*, Jersey Tulip; *New Mexico*, Santa Fe Trail; *New York*, Empire Star; *North Carolina*, Carolina Lily; *North Dakota*, Prairie Queen; *Ohio*, Ohio Star; *Oklahoma*, Cherokee Rose; *Oregon*, Union; *Pennsylvania*, Philadelphia Pavement; *Rhode Island*, Maple Leaf; *South Carolina*, Carolina Favorite; *South Dakota*, Gold Brick; *Tennessee*, Tennessee; *Texas*, Texas Bluebonnet; *Utah*, Honeycomb; *Vermont*, Snowfall; *Virginia*, Virginia Stock; *Washington*, Basket of Apples; *West Virginia*, Rhododendron Leaves; *Wisconsin*, Wreath of Violets; *Wyoming*, Cheyenne.

Discovery—500 Years by Ruth Powers, Carbondale, Kansas. 1990. Cotton, silver lamé, satin. The idea of both past and present discoveries are sensationally combined in this eye-catching quilt that showcases a draped flag. "I wanted to show the old and the new," the artist says, "but I also wanted to get the flag on because the flag demonstrations were going on at the time and I wanted to reflect our history and pride in our flag." The result is a noble tribute to the flag and to the explorations and discoveries of the last five centuries. Fifty stars, one for each state, are expertly quilted in the side borders of the quilt, and a quilted eagle holds pride of place in the center of the top border. The flag presented the most problems in putting the quilt together, she recalls. Getting the drapery right and then holding it in place was difficult, and a near-disaster occurred one day when the quilter arrived home to find that her puppy had chewed a hole in the flag! "The hole is still there," she notes, "but it is hidden in the folds of the drapery." The Santa Maria and the waves on which it rides are done with variations on a clamshell design because this artist likes to use traditional patterns in combination with original designs. The waves also contain "charm quilt" patches—small pieces of fabric that quilters trade or share with each other. The ship and much of the background were pieced using the English paper method. She chose silver lamé for the space ship because she wanted a very contemporary look; soon after she had completed it, she attended a seminar where the speaker, a fabric expert, stated that in years to come, experts will still be able to recognize the quilts of the 1980s by the lamé fabrics used. Ruth Powers, who has been a quilter for only a little more than a year, is a member of the Kansas Capitol Quilters Guild. She taught herself to quilt because she wanted to make a wall hanging; to date, she has made five wall hangings and two full-sized quilts, some of which have been shown in local quilt-guild exhibitions. This is her first contest, and she entered because she found the theme intriguing and "I thought it would be fun to try!"

From Rockport—With Love by Linda Hogan, Rockport, Massachusetts. 1990. Cotton, beads. A quilted-montage celebration of her home town serves as a starting point for this artist's invitation to Columbus, in a letter attached to the quilt, to discover the town's amenities. The letter also acts as a tourist's guide to the scenes shown in the quilt, as this excerpt indicates: "Rockport is a quaint old fishing village on Cape Ann in Massachusetts. Historically, the town has been an active participant in several wartime skirmishes, exemplified by a cannonball in the steeple of one of our churches. Rockport is a seaside community, with our main industry being lobster fishing. Visiting beaches and shopping at Bearskin Neck are [important] activities to this town. Christmas is a special event, with a decorated Christmas tree in the town square for the children. Twin lighthouses on Thatcher Island off our coast have been a landmark for ships for years. This is a town that you will surely want to explore further as you travel to the New World." The artist has combined the best-known elements of the town—from the cannonball in the steeple to the fisherman's shack that is reputed to be the most frequently painted motif in the country (Rockport has long been a recognized haven for artists)—into a delightful collage that could entice the spirit of any explorer. She wanted, she says, to depict a variety of Rockport scenes, "starting at sunrise and moving throughout the day." She developed the quilt from a nine-by-twelve-inch drawing, giving each scene its own perspective, and the whole is bordered by a quilted rope pattern that helps to carry through the maritime theme. Linda Hogan, a resident of the area for fifty years, began to quilt in 1982, and because she has seven children and numerous friends and relations, her quilts are always in demand as wedding, birthday, and holiday gifts. If pressured, she notes, she can whip up a quilt on a sewing machine in a week, but hand work goes more slowly, and she completes about three quilts a year. She is president of the Crossroads Quilters and also active in the New England Quilters Guild.

Cuervo Grande by Sandra Townsend Donabed, Wellesley Hills, Massachusetts. 1989. Cotton blends, polyester blends, rayon, metallic thread, gold leaf on canvas, acrylic paint, beads. On a trip to the Southwest, the artist stopped at the desert museum outside of Tucson, Arizona, where a large flock of huge ravens—"twice as big as crows," she recalled—had gathered. The scene brought to mind an old Indian legend of how the Great Raven brings light to the world, and she later decided to use this set of images when she was creating the design sketch for her contest entry. To her, the design became "my own discovery of America, invoking as it does the vastness of the country and the amazing differences from one region to another." She already had the gold fabric—made up of gold leaf on canvas—and felt that the difficulties of working with this type of surface would be more than offset by its shimmering, reflective effect and its utility as a source of background illumination that would capture a sense of the unusual light qualities of the Southwest. The memory of a very dramatic photograph of one of her children framed by a window of a cathedral in Venice decided the use of stone blocks as a framing element here; some of the blocks were created from appliquéd fabric that was hand marbleized in the shades of a desert sky at dawn, others have subtle stitching. The trailing vine has leaves so constructed that they project from the surface of the quilt, a three-dimensional technique that the artist likes to employ in her work. Sandra Donabed has been sewing since she was five years old and studied art education as an adult, but when she realized the possibilities offered by combining sewing and art through quilting, "it was like being hit by a lightening bolt," she says, "a logical extension of what I had been doing." When she is heavily involved in a quilting project, she may quilt night and day—"I watch David Letterman and get it done!"—and her family has discovered that meals may be sketchy while the creative urge is on! The artist belongs to the New England Quilters Guild, the Arlington Quilters Connection, and a local guild in Wellesley.

Through Sunshine and Shadow by Elsie Vredenburg, Tustin, Michigan. 1990. Cotton, cotton/polyester. This artist recalls the day that her grandmother abruptly announced to a less-than-enthusiastic teenager, "You and I are going to make a quilt," and so began a life-long preoccupation with quilting. Now a grandmother herself, Elsie Vredenburg is a full-time professional quilter with several hundred quilts to her credit. This quilt, the second in an architectural series that she is now working on, depicts six types of barns set against a background done in the traditional Sunshine and Shadow pattern. (The first in the series featured lighthouses against an Ocean Waves background; it won grand prize in a U.S. Coast Guard 200th Anniversary Quilt contest in 1990.) The quilter writes, "My America is rural. These old barns symbolize for me a way of life that is rapidly changing and disappearing. Through sunshine and shadow (the good times and the bad) the farmer has been the backbone of America." She is from a family of farmers and has seen old barns dying; the quilt is one way to record them for the future. Each barn represents a regional style, and their details are based on book illustrations. The piecing was especially tricky, she notes, because she wanted the appearance of the barns to be as accurate as possible, and a lot of ripping out had to be done before she achieved the desired effect. The scrap background, with its gradual wash of color from light to dark and back again, was also a challenge. The bright red chintz of the inner border was used, the artist adds, because many Michigan barns are painted that color. Elsie Vredenburg keeps a quilting frame in her living room and recalls that her grandsons, aged three and four, were fascinated with the quilting process. While attempting to help their grandmother, they dropped a pair of scissors on the quilt but, after a few "heart-stopping" moments, it was determined that no damage had been done! The quilter helped to form the Michigan Quilt Network; she is also a member of the Michigan Quilters Guild, the North Star Quilters, and national quilting organizations.

Lilly's Tomorrow by Faye Labanaris, Dover, New Hampshire. 1990. Cotton, corduroy, silk, embroidery floss, Vellex. "This quilt," says the artist, "shows a little girl looking out beyond her home, wondering what tomorrow will bring. Her puppy looks adoringly into her eyes. She is his world, but her world lies ahead." The design was inspired by a greeting card showing a girl and her dog sitting on a hilltop and watching the sun set, but the artist added her own ideas from that starting point. The little girl depicted is Faye Labanaris's godchild Lilly, who, she notes, is very special to her. Both she and Lilly's parents hope that someday Lilly will discover those parts of the country and unique places that have a special meaning to them, and these are the scenes shown on the quilt—the Statue of Liberty, the New England coast, the Amish country, the Washington Monument, a carousel, Diamond Head in Hawaii, the Southwest. "The 'purple mountains' majesty, the amber fields of grain'—America is beautiful!" the artist states enthusiastically, and she wants Lilly to find its beauty also. It took the quilter four months to gather the right fabrics for the quilt, and she found that some hand-painting was necessary in order to get the effects desired, particularly in the sky and in the area representing the Painted Desert of the Southwest. The work went smoothly from thereon—except for the carousel. Initially, she had conceived of more horses, but a photograph of Lilly's mother's horse decided the artist on a one-horse carousel, and that solved her problem. A retired science teacher, Faye Labanaris still volunteers a sizeable amount of her time to the school where she worked, and a new science project was being implemented just as she began work on the quilt. "For a while, I was not sure that I could complete both," she says, but both were completed on time and successfully! The artist belongs to the Cocheco Quilters Guild, the New England Quilters Guild, and the American Quilters Society. Her skills made her a state winner in the Memories of Childhood contest; she has been included in many other shows, and her work has won ribbons at the Vermont Quilt Festival.

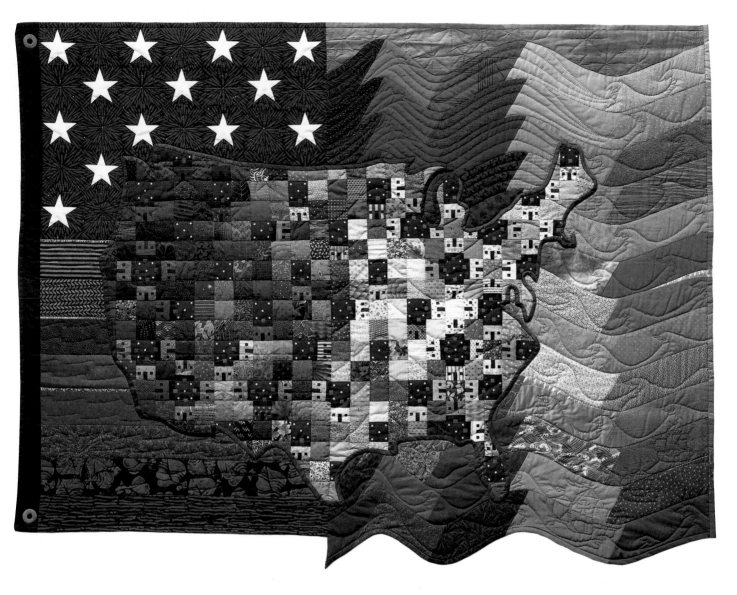

From Sea to Shining Sea by Jacqueline Paton, Merrimack, New Hampshire. 1990. Cotton, lamé, ultrasuede. In this dramatic reinterpretation of "Old Glory," the light of the rising sun shines on the eastern part of the country while stars still twinkle in the far west. The flowing stripes form the "purple mountains' majesty," which gradually, through line and color changes, become the "shining seas." "I love pictorial quilts," says this artist, "and I wanted the American flag to become a picture in my quilt." The map is composed of 331 patches, which include 288 different fabrics (the total fabric count for the whole quilt was 362 distinct prints and solids). Not only do the patches shade from light to dark, but the colors are cued to the region—for example, yellows and golds represent the grain belt; earth tones the deserts of the Southwest. The patches carry other information as well; some are done as tiny houses, and their placement indicates the density of population in a region. And, the quilter notes, "there is even a White House where the White House should be!" Alaska and Hawaii are not forgotten, either; polar bears are quilted in the upper left part of the quilt, and palm trees in the lower left. Color was a crucial key to the success of the quilt's design, and the artist found that she spent about a fifth of the time that she worked on the quilt in determining color placement. The binding on three sides also proved to be more time-consuming than expected because she wanted the binding fabric to match each interior piece that touched the edge, thus requiring a great deal of accurate piecing. The binding on the fourth side is intended to resemble the grommeted edge of an actual flag. In keeping with her overall theme, Jacqueline Paton wanted to finish the back of her quilt with a red, white, and blue section, but after cutting and piecing the back, she found that it had reversed itself and appeared blue, white, and red, which is the order of the colors in the French flag! The artist is a member of the New England Quilters Guild and the American Quilters Society. Her quilts have won awards at and have been exhibited in many different shows, and her work has been featured in magazines.

Discovering America: All That Glitters..." by Deborah Sarabia, Las Cruces, New Mexico. 1990. Cotton, cotton blends, metallic fabric. "The country is like a big crazy quilt, or a jigsaw puzzle, and it fits together just as it should," says this artist of her colorful entry that depicts a girl contemplating the placement of her next piece in this giant puzzle of the continental United States. The idea for the quilt design came to her when she saw a political cartoon of someone sitting over a map of the world and trying to rearrange it; "the idea just grew from there," she says. One of her goals was to represent the diverse nature of the country as well as the old and the new, and she used corporate logos, an Amish quilt block, what she terms "coyote kitsch," cows (for the dairy industry), and transportation and communication symbols to carry out this idea and to "show the great stuff about America." However, "in spite of all the glitter," she adds, "there are some basic problems that this country has yet to solve—poverty, the homeless, racism. These are in the embroidery underneath the surface of the puzzle [in the gray areas]." There are many other symbols used in the quilt as well: a maple leaf represents Canada, a pre-Columbian design Mexico, and Seminole piecing signifies the people here before Columbus. "As I was mailing the quilt for the contest," the artist recalls, "I realized that I had made a political statement as much as a quilt." Nevertheless, the quilt is lovingly and carefully crafted, right down to the detailed sole of the girl's sneaker and the friendship bracelet—made by the quilter's daughter—she wears on her wrist. Deborah Sarabia has been sewing since she was a child; although she knows both her grandmother and great-grandmother were quilters, she doesn't remember seeing them doing it and basically taught herself the techniques needed. Around 1981 she decided to try her hand at a crib quilt for her nephew and it has been a natural progression ever since. A member of the American Quilters Society and a very active person, she notes that she always has something going: "If it's not quilting, then I'm knitting or reading a book!"

Southwest Night Lights/New Mexico Nocturne by Jane Aruns, Sante Fe, New Mexico. 1990. All cotton. A stark black background sets the elements of a desert night off in sharp contrast as a full moon sparkles down on a sleeping pueblo and desert "critters" frolic to the melodic howls of a lone coyote in this inventive quilt that celebrates the discovery and beauty of the landscape of the Southwest. "I hope that the people who see this quilt get a sense of the uniqueness of the area," says the artist, who grew up in Missouri and is still discovering the diversity of her present home. "It's sort of fanciful out here; life forms are more subtle," she notes. "What appears to be a semi-arid desert in fact teems with life." And this is indeed the feeling that she has captured in this whimsical and colorful creation that shows native squash plants blossoming, cactus eagles soaring, long-eared jack rabbits romping, and reptiles slithering. She also wanted to capture the feeling of the unusual desert light through the colors in the central fan design of the quilt. Almost none of the colors repeat; they range from the very pale, through the jewel-like, to earthy tones; some are prints rather than solids to give a sense of the light filtering down from the moon. As she began to make the quilt, the design seemed to become much more complex than her original idea; "I spent two full months on appliqué alone!" she recalls. Jane Aruns, a member of the Northern New Mexico Quilters Guild, the New Mexico Quilters Association, the American Quilters Society, and the National Quilters Association, has won many awards for her quilts. Although she grew up thinking that quilts were special—she remembers a "Sunday Best" quilt that was brought out only on special occasions (her mother had made it when she was sixteen)—she did not begin to quilt seriously until 1979, even though she had learned to sew and embroider as a child. She is also encouraging this tradition in others; six neighborhood children, ranging in age from five through eleven (including two boys) were avid followers of her progress on this quilt—and now she is teaching them all to embroider!

A New Beginning by Donna Miska, Horseheads, New York. 1990. All cotton. This quilt not only shows Columbus's flagship riding the crest of the ocean waves but also is full of symbolism of what is yet to come as a result of his discovery. The thirteen stars represent the future colonies, the hints of red and white the stripes of the American flag; the skyline of a future city is nestled in the curve of the rainbow that arches over the ship, and a golden ring representing a wedding band encircles the ship, thus symbolizing the marriage of the Old World to the New. The brown and green calico prints in the lower part of the quilt represent the fertile land of the New World, and the blue fabric its rushing rivers. The sun also forms an abstract eye, connoting the watchful eye of God on the ship full of travelers. The quilt is a parable for growth and prosperity, or what America was to become. Although Donna Miska, a commercial artist by profession, has won several awards for her paintings, most of her quilts have been utilitarian, and this is the first quilt contest that she has entered. A neighbor had encouraged her to go to the Memories of Childhood exhibition at the last Great American Quilt Festival in 1989, and she found herself very excited by the quilts from an artist's point of view. Over lunch, she found herself thinking about the theme for this contest and immediately envisioned the Santa Maria at sea. She decided to go with that first inspiration—"you know in your heart when its your direction to go," she says. On the bus ride home from the quilt show, the driver got lost and so, she recalls, "I had a lot of time to think the idea through!" She knew basic quilting, but she felt that she did not know enough about its fine points, so she spent three months reading every quilt book she could find to educate herself about quilting. The idea for the quilt came faster than the execution, she says; "Painting is much quicker; quilting is very time-consuming." She dyed some of the fabrics herself, as she felt that the color selection in 100% cottons was very limited. "From an artist's point of view," she says, "I was very concerned with color overall."

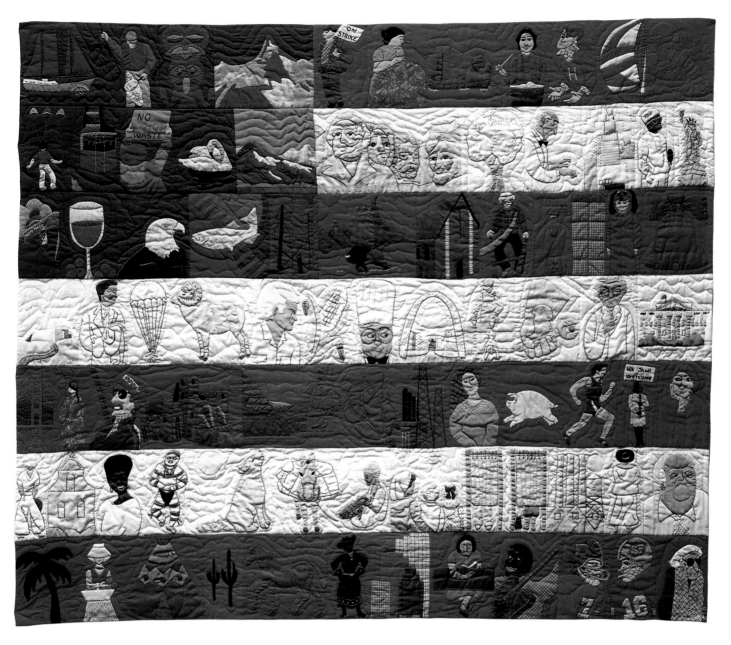

Exploring the Lower Forty-Eight by Patti Elwin Davis, Ithaca, New York. 1990. Cotton, cotton polyester, ultrasuede, silk. *Imaginative Use of Detail.* This delightful quilt has a map (of sorts) of the United States superimposed on a modified American flag, and appliquéd and embroidered in their approximate geographical setting are, according to the artist, "some of the landmarks, landscapes, and people representing our rich and varied multicultural heritage." The inspiration for the quilt came from a two-month trip Patti Davis and her husband took two years ago, driving from New York to California and back. As she describes it, "Driving westward, we followed the route of the Lewis and Clark expedition of 1804, and returning eastward, we explored the canyons, deserts, bayous, and beyond of the Southwest and the South. For someone like me, who has spent most of my life clinging to the eastern seaboard, it was an unforgettable experience. This wonderful trip set the theme for my quilt." The quilter wanted to express America's varied landscape and its "melting pot" aspect through the images she represented on her quilt, from the prosaic to the iconic. She regards Mount Rushmore as an important symbol of the greatness of the country and knew she had to include it, but she found it extremely difficult to depict the four presidents on its face; yet, because "it had to be right"— she worked hard to make all her figures realistic—she did it over until she was satisfied. She also felt compelled to make a statement about the polluted state of an otherwise beautiful land and used Greenpeace's ship, the Rainbow Warrior (located in the upper left corner of the quilt) and a woman holding a placard saying "No Hot Waste" to "express the temper of the times," she says. The artist spent seven months working on the quilt, and it came close to being destroyed one night when a raccoon came down the chimney and got into her quilting room. As luck would have it, the raccoon never touched the quilt, and she believes that it has had a "charmed life" since! Patti Davis, a member of the Ithaca Textile Arts Guild, has exhibited both nationally and locally.

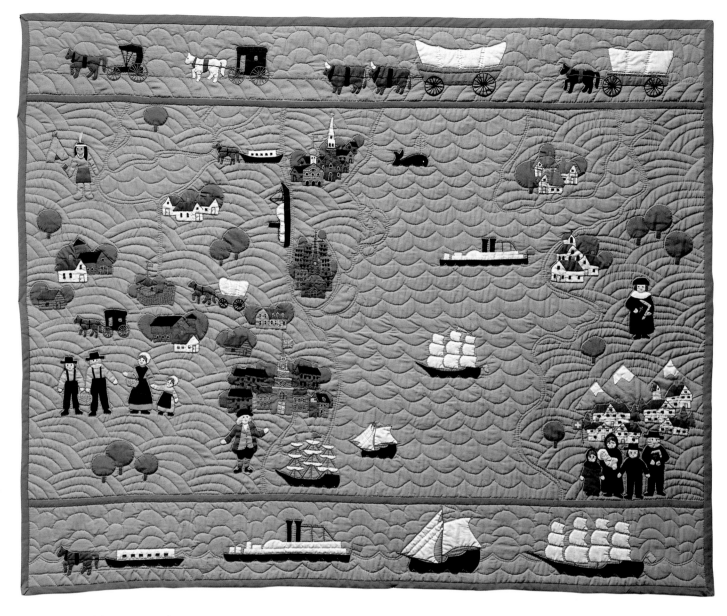

My Ancestors Coming to America 1717; 1733; 1833 by Joan Landis Bahm, New York, New York. 1990. Cotton and cotton blends. This charming compilation of people and continents is a documentary history of the artist's ancestors and their voyages of discovery to the New World over some one-hundred-plus years. Basically, "it is a map showing where different members of my family came from," she says, as well as a pictorial description of how they traveled and where they went. Joan Bahm has carried out a systematic genealogical study over the last ten or more years in order to learn more about her family, who originally came from Switzerland. From research in Switzerland through a careful review of the family records here, she has compiled a great deal of information, from the names of the ships they traveled on to dates of departure and arrival to final destinations. Her mother's grandmother, for example, was a Moravian who came to America in 1883, then went via the Erie Canal to Lake Erie, then traveled on the Ohio Canal to a settlement in New Philadelphia, Ohio. The many transportation symbols that border the quilt—steamships, sailing ships, canal barges and mules, covered wagons, Amish carriages—all indicate the many types of transportation used by her ancestors in the days when much of the country was, indeed, still a wilderness. She notes that William Penn was a significant figure in her family's history, as some of the early arrivals came here for religious freedom. "They were Old Order German, an offshoot of the Amish, and they were forced to leave Switzerland because of their religious beliefs," she recalls. "They then went to Germany and, when Penn opened Pennsylvania, it gave them the opportunity to come to America. They were here even before the Revolutionary War." Joan Bahm, a recognized folk painter, found both personal and professional satisfaction in making this quilt. The theme, she says, provided the initial inspiration, the design itself was an outgrowth of one of her genealogical paintings. Making the quilt allowed her to meditate on some of the varied and interesting aspects of her family's history.

The Eagle Has Landed by Catherine Bechtel, Columbiana, Ohio. 1990. Cotton, embroidery floss. "I love to be creative," says this quiltmaker, "and to do original rather than traditional designs." Her success is dramatically illustrated in this exciting design representing America rediscovered. "I feel as though there is a new era of discovery going on," she notes. "I am proud to be an American, and I guess it is mostly patriotism that is expressed here." The traditional symbols of the eagle and the flag that form the core of the design jut from a map of the United States far into a star-flecked space; the blue print border, with its delicate quilting, represents clouds. Once Catherine Bechtel decided to enter the contest, she spent months thinking about a possible design. "I knew I wanted to do something I liked, something contemporary, but I didn't quite know what. Finally, because I have strong religious beliefs, I asked the Lord to help me think of a design, and at two in the morning I woke up with a vision of the design in my head. I ran to the dining room and sketched what I had seen, and that's the quilt—there was nothing to change." Execution of the quilt required a great deal of technical expertise and preplanning; each feather on the underside of the eagle, for example, was individually appliquéd, one atop another, for a realistic look. The flagpole and flag also presented difficulties; the first being a matter of perspective, and the second a question of shape. In order to get the flag's furl to appear exactly as she wanted, the artist took a small flag, threaded a wire through the top, shaped it accordingly, and then used it as the model in making the pieced flag in the quilt. Initially, she was unsure whether she was going to use piecing or reverse appliqué for the background stars, but once she found the glowing star-studded fabric the choice was made. "Then I quilted another hundred or more stars around the printed ones to give it more depth," she notes. Catherine Bechtel, a musician by training, has been quilting for less than two years; she learned to quilt from two ladies at her local church, and this is only her second quilt.

Discovery Is What It's All About by Phyllis Bruce, Parma, Ohio. 1990. Cotton, metallic thread. In this intriguing interpretation of the contest theme, an umbilical-like cord stretches from the astronaut to an old-fashioned globe composed of tea-stained fabric, as though he were spawning a new creation. "I like making a statement," says the artist of her thought-evoking design, "and the contest theme—Discover America—lends itself to doing so. I believe that Americans are explorers, that America is on the forefront of space. And just as there is a need in all men to reach out and discover, I have a basic need as a quiltmaker to explore the surface of fabrics through quilting." The artist used Storm at Sea blocks as the quilt's border because she felt that it added to the idea of discovery and the multiple risks that discovery involves; she further enhanced this idea through the sense of expressed turbulence in the freehand quilting used in the border. She notes that she created her design in July 1989, soon after she knew about the contest, but waited nearly another four months before she actually began work on the quilt. "I was apprehensive about how a three-by-four-inch tablet drawing would translate to fabric in the larger size," she now recalls. She decided also to design the back of this quilt, because, she says, "I hate boring backs!" Thus, the reverse side of the quilt shows the back view of the astronaut, but the figure is carried out in brilliant splashes of color as opposed to the traditional white uniform used on the front. Phyllis Bruce, also a state winner in the 1987 Great American Liberty Quilt contest, has received many awards for her work. She is a member of a local quilt guild as well as the American Quilters Society and the National Quilters Association. "I am a fabricholic," she says. "I love every aspect of quilting, from the designing to the actual quilting." She started serious quilting in 1979, when she was an art instructor at a community center and taught a quilting class; there, she remembers, "I stayed only one step ahead of my students!" She is now activities coordinator in a nursing home and is teaching 80-year-olds to quilt.

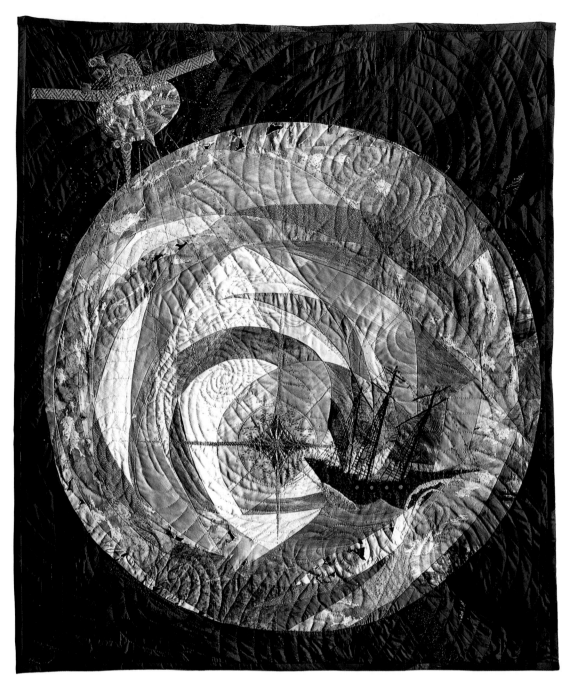

Spirit of Amerigo Vespucci by C. Jean Liittschwager, Leaburg, Oregon. 1990. Cotton, cotton blends, polyester, metallic fabric, metallic thread, beads. *Judge's Choice*. The planet earth forms the background for this quilt that is about exploration and discovery, as represented by a spacecraft, a compass, and a Spanish galleon. Additionally, notes the maker, it is about commerce in the world, as symbolized by the gold and silver threads and metallic fabrics. "These ongoing human endeavors and motivators—exploration, discovery, and commerce—were exemplified by America's namesake some 500 years ago and are still particularly pertinent in America today," she says. "Amerigo Vespucci was a business representative in Seville for the Medici family, and he worked for a company that outfitted ships, including those for two of Columbus's voyages. As the navigator himself on later voyages, Vespucci was responsible for the concept of a new continent with another ocean in between; he also developed a method of celestial navigation that resulted in a nearly accurate measure of the earth's circumference." The artist was inspired to create this design after a visit to Spain and Portugal, where Prince Henry once had a school of navigation. She looked for a place to buy material on this trip; but "because we didn't know the Spanish word for fabric, we ended up in a drapery shop!" She was captivated by the rich fabrics, however, and bought enough for the quilt anyway. She also notes that the colorful currency of the two countries reminded her of patchwork. She has used both fabrics and stitching in dynamic ways in order to represent the land, seas, atmosphere, and space, while selective beading further develops the idea of a generation and flow of energy—important components of discovery. The ship was the most trouble to make; she had to redo the embroidery for the rigging several times, and it is still not as good as she would like it to be. Jean Liittschwager, a member of the Pioneer Quilters, started quilting in 1987, after retiring from twenty-five years of teaching elementary school; she now spends some time every day at her quilting.

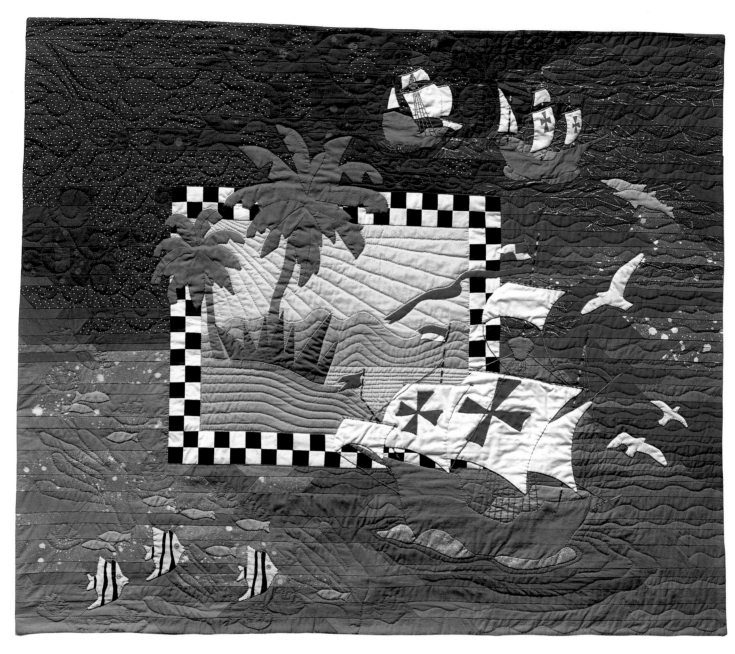

Trip to Discovery by Donna Albert, Lancaster, Pennsylvania. 1990. All cotton. The design, materials, and colors used in this quilt all serve to highlight the contrast between the long and difficult voyage that was faced by Columbus and his men in their crossing of the Atlantic and their arrival in a New World of vivid tropical lushness and life. "I wanted to get at the idea of coming out of the darkness of the voyage and old ideas into the sun of discovery," says the artist of her striking design, carried out through strip piecing, appliqué, and embroidery. The black-and-white border surrounding the central block, which depicts a simple landscape, creates a bold visual break between the warm and cool colors of the land, sea, and sky, and stitched swirls indicate, respectively, waves in the ocean and clouds and wind in the sky. Strange and unusual forms quilted into the blues representing the changing shades of the tropical ocean indicate the richness and diversity of the undersea life. The artist found that her design for this quilt had exceeded her hopes; "the first piece I made translated far better from the sketch into fabric than I had expected," she notes. Donna Albert, a textile designer by training, is a self-taught quilter; she likes quilting because "it just fascinates me to do something more spontaneous than weaving." From a beginning using traditional quilt designs, she has moved, as she says, to "taking off from there," and now she prefers creating her own designs. She has been strongly influenced by the Amish tradition so prevalent in the area where she lives. When she was learning to quilt, she participated in quilting bees run by a friend with Mennonite ladies, and she recalls her fascination with their work. "They made a lot of play with color," she notes, by contrasting, for example, yellow and orange with blue, producing simple yet highly effective color statements, and that is the impact that she wants her quilts to have. Donna Albert was a state winner in the Great American Liberty Quilt contest and has been featured in quilting books and in a book on fiber-arts design, which showed a series that she had based on an Amish design.

Stars of America by Louise Silk, Pittsburgh, Pennsylvania. 1990. Cotton. In a manner of speaking, says the quilter, the design of this quilt represents a group effort. As she thought about the piece and prepared her design, she conducted brainstorming sessions with everyone she met, asking the question, "What symbols do you think represent America?" Her question-and answer sessions, plus her involvement with Soviet immigration resettlement efforts in Pittsburgh, also helped the artist define what America meant to her. The wide-ranging results of her informal survey are to be found on the fifty stars arranged on this modified version of the flag (note the hint of stripes in the right-hand binding). She chose as many symbols as possible to express the diversity of America and the many things there are to discover about it, from the patriotic (a bald eagle and the Liberty Bell) to the homey (a turkey and, of course, a quilt) to the entertaining (Mickey Mouse and characters from "Sesame Street" and "Dr. Seuss") to icons of consumerism (Visa and MasterCard). Some symbols—such as those for Christmas—were ultimately rejected because their origins were not native to America. A baby reminiscent of Keith Haring's artwork was included in one of the stars not only to represent the contemporary art world, which the artist admires, but also as a symbol of AIDS, the disease from which Haring died. Louise Silk has found that she enjoys creating miniature images, but they do present some problems in execution because of their size—especially the more complicated ones, such as the Coca-Cola logo. In spite of the difficulties, she never relented in her determination to complete the quilt with all its myriad symbols; at times, she confesses, "the process becomes more important than the product!" Inspired by the idea of a charm quilt, in which no fabric is repeated, she also made certain that all the blues used as background were different. The artist, a professional quilter and a member of Associated Artists of Pittsburgh, the Fiber Arts Guild of Pittsburgh, and the American Quilters Society, has completed over 500 quilts, averaging about one a week.

31

Stone Carvings by Allison Stilwell-Cyr, Newport, Rhode Island. 1990. Cotton, jersey lamé, stencils, rubber stamps. The artist notes that this quilt, centered on petroglyph images carved on cave walls and ceremonial rocks many centuries ago by members of the Tiano and Arawak tribes in Puerto Rico, is dedicated to those Caribbean Indians whose people and cultures have been forever lost, in great part due to the European discovery of America. "History has been slanted in a certain way," she says. "It is important to me as a woman and as a fiber artist that my work makes people think and ask questions about things that have happened, even about times that were not happy ones for everyone." The second Great American Quilt Festival in 1989 "charged me up," she says, and provided the impetus to enter this contest. "I knew I wanted to do something with the Attic Windows pattern, something different," she recalls, "but I didn't know what. Finally, when a friend showed me notecards with pictures of the petroglyphs, I knew that 'This is it!'" She spent a great deal of time in the library researching the petroglyphs and the cultures that produced them, then had a difficult time deciding on which of the many petroglyph symbols to reproduce. "The quilt stood for a long time in pieces on the work wall—with empty windows," she remembers. The images, as noted in the stamped text on the quilt, represent many animal and human forms to which the Indians attached both magical and spiritual values. These starkly simply iconic designs are highlighted by the surrounding stitching and by the hand-painted background fabric that calls to mind something of the tropical brilliance of their natural environment. The three-dimensional effect produced by the Attic Windows pattern seems, appropriately, to lead the viewer back into time to gain a full appreciation of these unusual images. This is only the third quilt that Allison Stilwell-Cyr has made since she started quilting less than three years ago. She learned what she terms her "contemporary flair" from her sister, a fiber artist, with whom she currently shares a studio, and her quilting skills from the owner of a local quilt shop.

Haze at Sunset: East Tennessee by Marcia E. Sherrell, Newport, Tennessee. 1990. After a move from the urban flatlands of Indiana to the isolated highlands of Tennessee, this artist found herself "responding in awe to the movement of light and color in the mountains." Because of the move, she says, she rediscovered America "in our new land and a new way of life." Making the quilt became a project of love, as she attempted to show the spirit and beauty of her new home. "I wanted to reflect how the light dances on the mountains. Spring here is so intense, the blues so blue, the greens so green, the sky so transparent, with the haze creating a turquoise effect." Not only do the jewel-like tones capture that image, the texture of the quilt, through tucks and turns and "tidbits" of fabric that nestle in curves and corners, instills the viewer with the urge to reach out and touch. Three weeks before the contest deadline, the quilter found that she was so unhappy with what she had completed to date that she cut up the entire quilt and then reassembled it in its present form. After doing this, she notes, she experienced, a "great sense of relief and felt that everything then fell together!" The artist often thinks about the quilters of bygone days when she works. After moving, for example, she found herself surrounded by a mountain of still-packed boxes, and somewhere among them were her quilting materials. It might have saved her time and been easier to go out and buy what she needed for this quilt, but, as she recalled all those women of earlier days who had to make do with what they had, she decided to search out her box of fabrics and make do with what she had, too. Marcia Sherrell's interest in quilting goes back thirteen years, to the time when she was in the antiques business and, as an expert sewer, found herself mending quilts for other dealers. A former president of the Muncie Quilters Guild in Indiana, she is now, she admits, "obsessed" with quilting and usually has two going at once—"one on a frame and one in a basket near my chair!" "If I have five minutes to sit down," she says, "I begin to quilt."

This-n-That in the USA by Helen Giddens, Dallas, Texas. 1990. Cotton, shiny vinyl, acetate satin. Vibrant and divergent images scattered helter-skelter and held within the confines of a jagged border of triangles form a tangible textile signature of this artist. Her designs often start out as what she describes as "no more than doodles," then later she makes drawings from her "doodles" that she uses as patterns. Each of the figures used in the quilt is cut out separately and placed on the paper pattern; the quilter than stands back and looks at the proposed quilt as though it were a painting and makes sure that all the colors work together. In this quilt, which is entirely pieced, the artist has ingeniously arranged her images in a map-like manner in order to represent various regions of the United States. There are roller skates to represent a popular Los Angeles sport, a slot-machine window for Las Vegas, a bright and shiny automobile for Detroit, towering redwoods for the Northwest, the Alamo for Texas, a soaring golden arch for St. Louis, an alligator for Florida, a flag for the nation's capitol, and a sailboat for New England, while the buffalo and the teepee serve as "reminders of what used to be." In some of the motifs the fabric cleverly reinforces the image; snowmen and penguins, for example, can be found in the prints around the igloo representing Alaska. The happy face of New York's Statue of Liberty had to be redone three times, says the artist, because "it kept coming out looking sad or mean," not the image she wanted! Helen Giddens is a self-taught quilter who has perfected her skills through trial and error; she is also an artist whose work includes paintings and silkscreen prints. She has made over one hundred quilts in the sixteen years that she has been quilting and considers herself a studio quilt artist—"one who considers her quilting as an art," she says. She is a member of the Dallas Quilters Guild, the Studio Quilt Artists, the North Texas Quilt Artists, and the AIQA. Her work has been widely exhibited and won other awards, including the Memories of Childhood contest and the Artist as Quiltmaker show in Ohio.

The Other Side of the Ocean Sea by Mary Ann Herndon, Houston, Texas. 1990. All cotton. The cover illustration for the book *The Canary Who Sailed with Columbus* by Susan Wiggs inspired this delicately tinted pictorial quilt that features a bust-length portrait of a robust Columbus standing before the rigging of his ship's mast; stylized elements representing a compass, the continents, swirling waves, and blowing winds act as a frame for the imposing central figure. A blazing sun and softly smiling moon in the upper corners symbolize the main tools of navigation of the time; Columbus's three small ships bravely make their way through uncharted blue-green seas at the upper edge of the frame, and a half-seen anchor at the bottom seems to hold the whole composition in place. The wonderfully colorful tropical fish blowing bubbles in the three borders of the quilt were cut from a piece of fabric depicting an underwater scene and appliquéd here to carry through the nautical theme, and the intricate quilting enhances the sense of strong air and ocean currents. Mary Ann Herndon, a district coordinator of school libraries, was initially attracted by the contest theme but she had some reservations about entering—not least of them being whether a full-time job and the demands of three growing children would allow the needed time to complete the quilt! However, she notes, she is basically a competitive person (she was a state runner-up in the Memories of Childhood contest) and so decided to go ahead with the goal of winning this time. Mary Ann Herndon has "always been interested in fabrics"; she had long done needlepoint and embroidery, then added quilting to her repertoire after learning it at a local store ten years ago. Her busy schedule has not allowed her to devote as much time as she would like to quilting, but she has done enough to have her work featured in a book on Texas quilts, in two quilt calendars, and in the *Quilter's Newsletter Magazine* in 1987. The artist, an active member of the Houston Quilt Group, has done traditional patterns but prefers to devote her limited time to making quilts and wall hangings based on her own original designs.

America's Youth on the Threshold of Discovery by Linda M. Pool, Vienna, Virginia. 1990. All cotton. In this charming composition, two children sit at the threshold of their own homely world and consider all there is to discover in the future in the world beyond their doors. "They are looking out at what our country, in all its beauty, has to offer," the artist says. Perhaps the children are also considering the intriguing puzzle that Linda Pool has worked into the quilt for the clever viewer to find—eight animals are hidden somewhere within the quilt itself! She notes that her design was initially inspired by a greeting card showing two children looking out to sea. "I was in Colorado at the time, and so I used mountains instead," says this artist, recalling how impressed she had been by the excitement and the grandeur of the western landscape, a vision she still recalls with pleasure. She particularly wanted to achieve a realistic and dimensional perspective for the outdoors scene, and did this through the fabrics she used and through her quilting techniques. Execution, she says, was much harder than coming up with the design, particularly in fitting the sky, mountains, and grass into the panes of the French doors; "I wasn't sure everything was going to hold together," she now recalls. Linda Pool teaches and lectures regularly on quilting, when she is not handling the bookkeeping for her husband's business or working on her own quilting projects. She remembers that her grandmother had quilted all her life, and when this artist decided that she wanted to continue the tradition, she set out to teach herself. "I mailed away for a quilt kit and received a kit for an appliqué quilt. I didn't even know what appliqué was at the time!" The quilter has come a long way since then. She is a former president of her chapter of Quilters Unlimited, and she has exhibited at and won awards in a number of different shows; she was also a winner in the Memories of Childhood contest. When she heard of this contest, she decided to try again; "I like a challenge. I liked the theme, I came up with an idea, and I wanted to go with it!"

America Discovered Through Quilts: Past, Present, and Future by Jean A. Natrop, Mayville, Wisconsin. 1990. All cotton. Quilts upon quilts flow through the generations in this piece, recording the histories of the country and its families, all to be discovered and rediscovered by the generations to come. A figure in nineteenth-century garb represents the past, a modern woman the present, and a baby girl—a Sunbonnet Sue—the future. In a sense, the design represents the heritage of the American people, what each family has brought to the country, how patterns may change, yet remain unchanged through the years. "The quilt made me think about women working today on the same patterns that were used a hundred or more years ago, and I wondered if we think of the same things now as they thought about then," the artist meditates. Some of the fabrics used in the quilt were antique, ranging from the turn of the century to the 1930s; these were obtained at auctions or from other participants in her church quilting bees. Others were very new and contemporary because, she notes, "I wanted to typify the history of quilting, of fabrics being passed from one generation to another." The antique fabrics are found in the woman of the past, while the small child, representing the future, is made with the newest fabrics and quilting techniques. At one point, it seemed the quilt would never make it to the judging for the contest. "The day before the slides had to be mailed, the film shop lost them," Jean Natrop recalls. However, she managed to photograph a second set and get them developed and mailed in record time! Her mother and both grandmothers were quilters, but all had died before this artist began to teach herself to quilt— "although I might have learned something through osmosis," she acknowledges. She has now made over 300 quilts. "For fourteen years I've been cranking them out," she says. "It's my business." She has just completed twenty quilts for a local bed-and-breakfast inn; five are original designs, and all have an Audubon (the name of the inn) theme. Her work has won awards in other state and national contests as well.

Discover America: If Columbus Could See Us Now by Jean Teal, Oconomowoc, Wisconsin. 1990. Cotton, netting. Although this artist's interest in American history and especially the Revolutionary War, sparked by the musical *1776*, is reflected in this quilt through the images of Independence Hall and an early flag, her primary motif is a record of the systematic environmental destruction of the country from the time of Columbus's coming to the present. As she says, "from the pure to pollution" in only five hundred years, from the pristine sands and towering forests to oil-stained beaches and encroaching concrete landscapes. There is some irony in the fact that green is her favorite color, and that color symbolically disappears from the quilt as the grays, browns, blacks, and other darker hues of pollution become more prominent as the pieced and appliquéd design moves through the years. All the detrimental environmental signs of our time are revealed in the quilt— the cooling towers of Three-Mile Island, trees destroyed by acid rain, a dead whale, trains carrying huge redwood logs, an oil spill, and a "mucky-looking" patch of landfill. Perhaps closest to home for this artist is the tractor pulling a tank of liquid fertilizer, which has been a source of water and well pollution in her home town. The design was based on some rough sketches, but most of the images, the quilter notes, were done freehand and the "work just grew." The evergreen trees near the Indian teepees are cutouts, with the branches left loose to make them more realistic. Jean Teal says that in some respects finding the time to work was the hardest part of making this quilt. She was in the midst of selling her home and moving, and she had to quilt during all the resultant "confusion and chaos." On the bright side, however, she says being able to concentrate on the quilt probably helped to "keep her sane!" The artist, a self-taught quilter, is a member of the Pine Tree Needlers and Wisconsin Quilters Inc. A state winner in the Memories of Childhood contest, this artist also won an Honorable Mention in the 1990 National Quilters Association show and has had her work widely exhibited.

Renovated Cabin by Christopher King, Baddeck, Nova Scotia, Canada. 1990. Raw silk, cotton felt. "One can do something with a visual image that can't be done with words," says this artist; he wanted this brilliant quilt to stimulate the viewer to "look at the world and rediscover what it means." On a more literal basis, the quilt represents Nova Scotia, with its extensive forests and ocean borders, and the cabin itself is the home that Christopher King was in the process of renovating. The traditional Log Cabin pattern is used in his design but, as he says, it is "turned on its head," thus giving the opportunity to reconsider its many possibilities. The quilt is constructed of nearly 2000 pieces of raw silk, hand-dyed in startling and vivid colors, which have been placed "to spark off each other...to do something wonderful." In a sense, the quilt is an allegory; just as diverse racial and ethnic groups are juxtaposed in the world, the artist has juxtaposed wildly divergent colors that yet create an overall harmonious effect. Thus the quilt is a symbol of his dream that "new colors and patterns will manifest themselves in the nineties," providing new hope for the future of mankind. The artist, a commercial tree planter who quilts when he can after work and throughout the long, cold, and snowy winter months when planting is impossible, finds that working with bright colors provides "an antidote to the external gray and white landscape of snow." Christopher King has long been interested in fabric and has made his own clothes. He was introduced to quilts in an antiques store in London twenty years ago and then began making quilts for himself. As a member of the Nova Scotia Designer Craft Council, he is very much involved in the fiber-arts field in Nova Scotia and sometimes finds himself pondering the thin boundary between a work of fiber art and a quilt not made for utilitarian purposes. In 1989 he brought a group from Nova Scotia to The Great American Quilt Festival, and he claims that he had never before been in a place with so many women around him. Although "a bit overwhelmed," he admits to "enjoying the company!"

Discover America in the Nature by Hanne Wellendorph, Vemmelev, Denmark. 1990. Cotton, batik, silk, synthetics. "Discover your own private America through nature," urges this artist. "Do like the insects—put your wings on, start your engine, be like the 'busy bee'! Stop at the first wild rose. Discover warmth, friends, your heritage by sitting, humming, feeling with your soul…discover and conquer this world by keeping your eyes open—and don't forget to bring the nectar home!" The inspiration for this bright design came as she sat in the middle of a field of wild flowers at her summer home, and she notes that many of the parts of the rose in her quilt incorporate traditional American patterns: Tumbling Blocks, Log Cabin, Schoolhouse, and Grandmother's Flower Garden hexagons, for example. The Amish horse and buggy, as well as the Diamond in a Square, is a tribute to a part of America that she much admires. The quilt has an international flavor as well, for the fabrics used are from Denmark, America, and China. The artist, a three-time visitor to the United States, vividly describes her own reactions to this country: "I feel like a busy bee the very moment I put my feet on American ground. The more I discover, the better I feel and the more I want to discover—more friends, more American folk art, more Baltimore Album quilts, more quilting people, more American heirlooms." Hanne Wellendorph describes herself as a "patchwork ambassador"; she has taught English piecing in the United States, and she was instrumental in starting a quilting movement in Denmark (which had no quilting tradition) by founding a patchwork club that currently has over two hundred members throughout the country. Her ideas have received even more exposure through five books on patchwork that she has written and through television appearances and a slide show, also on patchwork. The artist is a self-taught quilter who is constantly at work on new quilting projects, many of which are illustrated in her books. She has exhibited her work internationally, and she was the Third Place Grand Prize Winner in the Memories of Childhood contest.

Navigare Nelesse Est, or Dream Big by Mirja Muurinen, Puskiaistentie, Finland. 1990. Cotton, cotton blends. For this artist, "there is no sense in searching for new things far away. Discovery is right there, hidden within ourselves." The idea of new visions for oneself inspired her design for this quilt. Because she was interested in circles, she took that form as the dominant idea for the design, using a central round medallion with concentric rings to symbolize the world, and including a symbolic rudder to signify the concept of navigation, or the need to steer one's self through life. The darker strips represent mental obstacles that must be overcome if desired goals are to be accomplished. This highly abstract presentation of a number of fundamental and important concepts is carried out against a background of one-patch blocks in a graduated palette of color and pattern that, in conjunction with the swirling print of the border, brings a luminous sense of energy and motion to the quilt. The elements used in the quilt top also are reminiscent of the kind of work and materials found in ancient Finnish cloth rugs. Although the artist learned about the Discover America contest only last summer, the theme interested her—probably, she notes, "because of the big discovery in my life: quilting!"—and she thought that the smaller size required by the contest rules made it feasible for her to complete the quilt by the deadline. Thus, she got to work and managed to finish the quilt, from design through the last stitch of quilting, within a month. "There was no time for problems or for getting discouraged about the quilt," she recalls. A founder and the president of the first Quilters Guild in Finland, Mirja Muurinen has been quilting for about seven years. Because there is no quilting tradition in her family, she is mostly self-taught; "I ordered books, magazines, fabrics, and *Quilter's Newsletter Magazine* for learning," she recalls. This busy mother of four young children—she also teaches English to adults at a local school—participated in the Quilt Expo Europa in Salzburg and attended the International Quilt Festival in Houston in 1989.

My First Impression of America by Noriko Isshiki, Chibashi, Japan. 1990. Silk, cotton, lace. The quilt design is based on the artist's experiences in and impressions of this country after her first visit to the United States two years ago, when she came to attend The Great American Quilt Festival as a runner-up in the Memories of Childhood contest. Some of the memorable sights for her as depicted on her quilt were the Statue of Liberty, the Capitol building in Washington, and the skyscrapers of New York City. Captured in a circle on the quilt, as though seen through the porthole of a ship, are cherry blossoms, which were in bloom during her visit. She also decided to include in her composition "an old sailing boat, which is meant to be the boat on which Columbus sailed to America." She was worried about how to do justice to Columbus's difficult voyage in the quilt format. "I wondered how I could depict the rough waves," she says, but she solved the problem through a careful combination of piecing, quilting, and color choice that has produced a wonderfully turbulent effect. Noriko Isshiki notes that some of the materials used in the quilt had been left to her by her mother, who died at the age of ninety-nine. She also included the fabric from a kimono that she had worn when she was young. "These fabrics mean a lot to me," she says; "therefore, rather than wasting them, I wanted to use them for something meaningful." Some of the fabrics she dyed herself, and she has incorporated elements of both Japanese and American quilting techniques to stunning effect in the overall execution of the quilt. She recalls that she did not draw out her design for the Memories of Childhood contest but rather designed as she quilted; this time, however, she decided to sketch out her ideas ahead of time so that all the elements would be carefully planned and incorporated into the final design. "Since I am not very good at designing," she says, "my husband, who likes to paint, gave me occasional but very useful advice!" Noriko Isshiki learned to quilt in 1983 through a combination of private lessons and self-teaching; she is a member of the Friendship Quilters.

Happy Memory by Etsuko Sugita, Hirakata, Osaka, Japan. 1990. Cotton, synthetic fiber, cotton embroidery yarn. *Best International Entry.* A collage of bright images captures the artist's memories of a 1989 visit to and discovery of America with her daughter. She recalls a wide range of experiences, from riding in yellow cabs to seeing *Cats* to visiting the Empire State Building and other parts of the Big Apple to touring rural areas. "I created my own version of the Statue of Liberty, one with Marilyn Monroe's face, who, instead of holding a torch, holds an ice cream cone," she says, "because I enjoyed American ice cream so very much!" A series of Humpty-Dumpties falls from the Big Apple at the center as a tribute to Columbus's use of a boiled egg to prove the value of finding unique rather than conventional ways of making things happen. "Because of his creative approach to things," the quilter says, "he could discover America." The quilt makes use of a happy hodgepodge of appliqué, piecing, embroidery, and Crazy quilting that adds to its colorful charm and liveliness. Etsuko Sugita says that her education, work, and hobbies have always been closely connected with fabric. A trained dress designer, she was inspired to begin making quilts after reading a book on the Shelburne Museum's quilt collection. "I was very impressed by the beauty of the work," she recalls, and so began to teach herself to quilt. A member of the Japan Quilters Association, she now spends as much time as possible making quilts and holds private classes in quilting at her home. Her schoolteacher husband has become fascinated by quilts, too, and for the last two years has been making traditional American-style quilts, some using Amish designs. This is the first original design the artist has attempted; her other quilts have all also been based on traditional American patterns, but in this one she decided she wanted a special design in order to commemorate her visit. Before she began the design, the artist looked at all the photographs from her trip, and she and her daughter (both of whom are shown on the American flag on the quilt) had a good time remembering their lighthearted discovery of America!

New York, New York by Hiroko Nakamura, Toyohashi, Aichi, Japan. 1990. Cotton, silk, synthetics. Skyscrapers, musicals, yellow cabs, and a busy night life are some of the elements that comprise this artist's discovery of America after a visit here in 1989. She came to attend the second Great American Quilt Festival and decided then that she wanted to participate in the contest for the third Quilt Festival. "I liked the theme, because my trip gave me a better idea of what America is," she says. She was happy with the required size of the quilt, too, because she felt that it was an appropriate size for the expression of her idea. "Since I had enjoyed the musical *Black and Blue*, I wanted to make a quilt that had movement and rhythm." Also, she adds, "America gives me an impression of brightness and cheerfulness. Although my quilt depicts night life, I wanted to express those themes in it, too." This particular quilt is unique among her usual work because of the materials; normally she uses only silk kimono fabrics in her quilts, but this time she included some synthetic fabrics in order to capture a sense of the brightness and illumination of a lively New York night. Her fabric choices, she notes, are probably tied to her upbringing; "My father is a craftsman who works as a traditional *yuzen* kimono dyer in Kyoto. When I was young, I was always surrounded by silk fabrics and beautiful colors, which influenced me then and are still influencing me and my work today." Hiroko Nakamura began quilting nearly twenty years ago, soon after a friend gave her a book on quilts as a souvenir of her visit to America. "Since I was very impressed by the work," she says, "I started making quilts by myself." The artist believes that this quilt and the contest gave her many new quiltmaking experiences; she was challenged by the theme, by the use of new materials, and by a new technique—this is the first quilt on which she has used appliqué—and through these, she had new opportunities to discover herself. The artist has won a number or prizes for her work in Japan, and she has been included in many exhibitions in Japan and elsewhere.

How Would You Like to Cook, Columbus? by Sachiko Shimomura, Yokohama, Kanagawa, Japan. 1990. All cotton. *Judge's Choice.* This lively and whimsical quilt is a fanciful interpretation of a well-known anecdote about Columbus and a boiled egg. When Columbus wished to gain support for his proposed voyage to discover a new route to the East, so the story goes, he faced a number of disbelievers in the Spanish court whose imaginative abilities were trapped by the boundaries of the conventional wisdom of the time. In an effort to prove that new ideas were needed, Columbus gave a hardboiled egg to some members of this group and asked them to make it stand upright. No one could do this, and when the egg was returned to Columbus, he promptly tapped the egg against a table to make the bottom flat, thus enabling the egg to stand upright and so proving his point that new and unconventional methods must be used if new discoveries were to be made. "Usually," says the artist, "I don't think about a theme before making a quilt, I just make a design that I like. I don't want to confine myself, whether I use an original design or a traditional design. Thus, this quilt is a unique piece for me, made as it was to correspond to a set theme." The stars and stripes may be traditionally American, but the concept and presentation is uniquely the artist's own. It took her one month to create the design and five months to complete the piecing, appliqué, and quilting—and, she says, "it was difficult to depict eggshells realistically!" She notes that her image of America is a country that maintains its strength with a positive and clear attitude, and, she says, she created this quilt with much the same attitude in mind, completing it in an atmosphere of energy, cheerfulness, and enjoyment. Sachiko Shimomura spent nine years in the United States and learned the basics of quiltmaking while she was here. After her return to Japan, she founded the Japan Quilters Association in 1987, and it now has over 160 members. She also translated the entry form for Discover America into Japanese in order to encourage Japanese quiltmakers to participate in the contest.

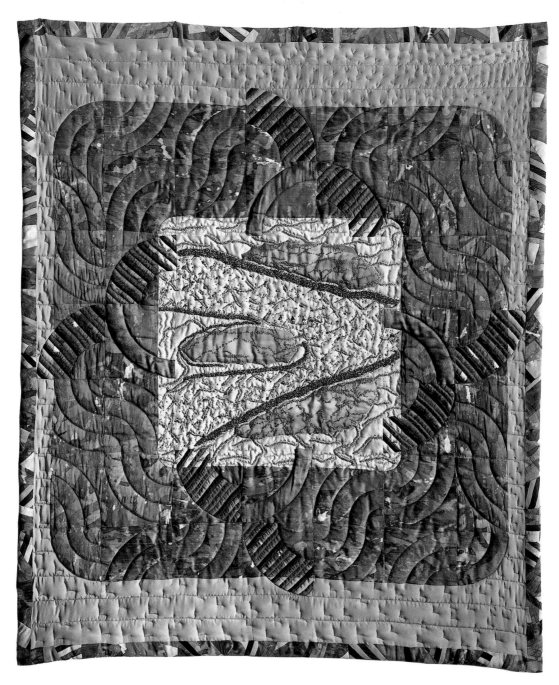

Florida's Seas by Nelleke van de Wege-van Sevenhoven, Lucaswolde, The Netherlands. 1990. Silks, including satin, shantung, pongee, granité. A trip to the Long Key State Recreation Area in Florida provided the artist with inspiration for this quilt. She writes: "The colors of Florida's seas were a real discovery for me. I had never seen such beautiful colors before—in Europe, you don't see these turquoise tints. I simply had to make a quilt based on this." She also notes that "sailing these waters must have been a great thrill in the time of Columbus because there weren't any blocks of flats then spoiling the view!" The artist says that she became obsessed with translating to the quilt the colors she had captured in her memory and in photographs and found that hand-dyeing offered the only solution to getting the purity of the hues she recalled. She also used heavy and light, textured and smooth silks to add texture, structure, and emphasis to each area of her quilt. The pools, for example, were done with pongee, the sandy beach with shantung, the seas in Indian silk, the tree trunks in granité, the palm leaves in pieced strips of pongee broché, and the sky in a pale, shimmering satin. She has used embroidery to great dimensional effect in the areas representing grass on the beach and in the flock of dainty shore birds huddled together. The piecing and quilting further amplify the overall impact, in the curving seams that enhance the illusion of waves in the sea, the small stitches done in different colors on the "sand" that give the impression of miniscule shells, and the quilted bird silhouettes that are intended, the artist says "to break the monotony of a clear sky on a hot summer day." The artist notes that one goal in making this quilt was to enable the viewer to "stand in front of it, in the light, and have the beach and the water come alive." Nelleke van de Wege-van Sevenhoven, a home economics teacher, has been "hooked" on quilting since she began five years ago but has to "steal" time in her busy life to do it. She is a member of the Dutch Quilters Association and has had her work exhibited in both Europe and the United States.

Dimensional Discoveries by Janet Grey-Inglis, Taupo, New Zealand. 1990 All cotton. "This collage of the U.S.A. shows how an outsider like myself sees the country and the reasons we would want to 'discover' it today," says the artist of her colorful and zesty design. "One of the main ways we discover your country is via the movie industry, hence the large filmstrip—this is also one of the U.S.A.'s attractions for us." She has included a variety of historical, geographical, and cultural facets of the country in her design. It is a complex and many-leveled presentation, starting with a border representing exploration by sea, through the westward movement by covered wagon through California gold and fertile farmland. Not only has she captured some element of each of the diverse areas of the country—mountains, prairies, swamps, rivers, deserts, and megalopolises ("unimaginable and awesome, especially when perceived from a country the size of mine," she notes) through color, shapes, and quilting. She has also included a sampling of the melting pot of characters that comprise it, such as oilmen, ranchers, sheriffs, sunbathers, movie stars, and different ethnic groups. This is the artist's first entry in an international contest, and she was attracted by the theme. "It looked like a challenge—and you want to extend yourself," she notes. Her experience as a geography teacher at a local college served her well in developing the design for the quilt as she worked to capture a sense of the vast panorama of America. The artist's quilting expertise evolved from an earlier interest in tile decorating, which had led to a desire to try her hand at patchwork; she soon found, however, that nontraditional themes were more interesting—"I refuse to do things that are too simple," she says. The artist used a range of techniques, from patchwork to embroidery to hand-dyed fabric, to create the very special effect produced by this quilt. Janet Grey-Inglis, a member of the Taupo Quilters Group, has one of her quilts in the permanent collection of a local museum. She hopes someday to be able to discover America personally, and not only through films and books.

Georgetown: Azaleas in Blossom—Impressions of My First Visit to the USA in April 1990 by Natalia Kuksina, Moscow, U.S.S.R. 1990. Cotton, cotton blends, synthetics, lace, buttons. "If I had not visited the United States," says artist, who has a love affair with nature, "I probably would have used the skyscrapers of Manhattan in designing my work. What most surprised me about America were the singing birds and the smell of fresh-cut grass in the country's capital city. I was most impressed not by the unusual architecture of New York City and the richness of its museums, nor by modern technology and automobiles, but by the quiet streets of Georgetown, where the snow-white houses were surrounded by green lawns, with windows almost hidden behind blooming azaleas of many colors from white to deep, rich purple-reds. Georgetown—where the historic channel [the old C & O barge canal] with wooden bridges across it is surrounded by violet gloxinias, where the red-brick houses and Georgetown University are shadowed by blooming dogwoods. I wanted to show the wood and brick of the houses, the green shadows of the lawns, and, most of all, the beauty of the flowers in blossom." That the artist has been successful in translating to fabric the images that she has so graphically described is in no doubt; the quilt fairly shimmers with light and color. Hand-dyed fragments of lace and brilliant scraps of fabric are all combined in a glowing collage that captures the essence of spring in one of our country's loveliest urban areas. Half-hidden houses, presented both pictorially and in the abstract through use of a brick-like fabric, seem to peek through the flowering riot of color, and an intricately tucked and turned border provides additional depth and dimension to the overall design. Natalia Kuksina, whose background and training is in costume and theatre decoration, has worked for the Bolshoi Theatre. This is her first quilt, and, she notes, "I spent most of my life painting landscapes, and I approached this work as a painter [in terms of color and design]." Her work provides quilters here with an insight into the concepts and techniques in quilting now current in the U.S.S.R.

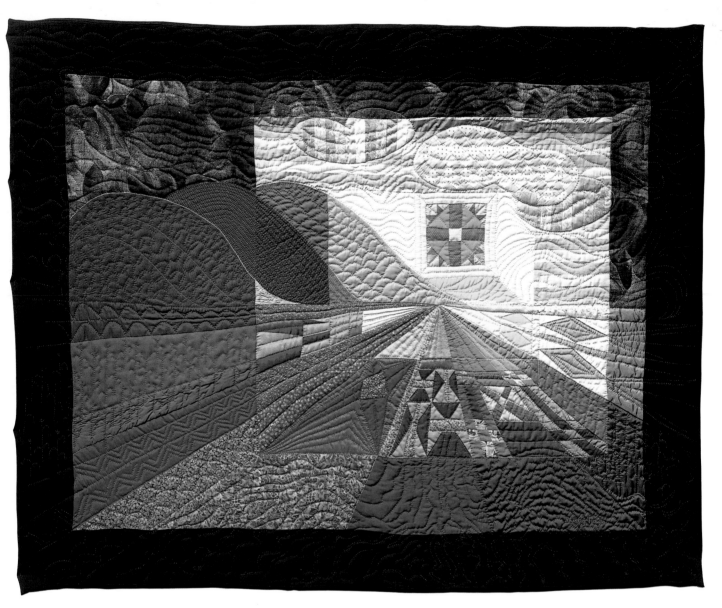

Crossroads by Shirley Herzer, Grünstadt, West Germany. 1989. Cotton, synthetics. In this quilt, an imaginary landscape that calls to mind the endless plains of the West meets towering mountains at the horizon. "It is a landscape, and inside that landscape is a landscape that is also a color wheel. Outside that square, the colors recede in their intensity," the artist says. The sun is depicted as the traditional Cross and Crown patch, "which has a theological meaning that 'Christ is the Light of the world'," she notes. The fields below also contain within their elongated perspective old and familiar patchwork motifs, all relating to road or travel symbolism—Road to Oklahoma, Arkansas Traveler, World Without End, Missouri Puzzle, and Garden of Eden. Many of the quilting patterns, diverse in themselves, were inspired by Indian symbolism. Although Shirley Herzer had already started this quilt when she heard about the contest, she felt that it fit right into the theme and so decided to enter it. "I thought the colors, the quilting, and the idea were very American, and, through the perspective, I wanted to draw the viewer into the American landscape, to become a part of it. It was also an expression of my homesickness." She had, she says, walked around for two months with the design for the quilt in her head before she actually put it down on paper. Several of the fabrics used in the quilt are pieced from materials from her mother and mother-in-law, which gives it an additional layer of meaning for the artist. Shirley Herzer, an American married to a German, carried a quilting tradition with her when she left this country. She is self-taught, although she remembers watching her mother and grandmother quilt. She was asked to give a course in patchwork in Germany, "so I got a book and learned to teach quilting," she recalls. "At least I would be an hour ahead of the students!" From that point, she just never stopped quilting, and she now has made around twenty-five quilts. She is a member of Patchwork Gilde, a national quilters group in Germany, and of a local quilters group; her work was also included in the Visions of the World exhibition in Salzburg.

Five Hundred Years, New Ideas by Inge Schulz-Loeffler, Leopoldshohe, West Germany. 1990. Cotton, dacron polyfill. *Judge's Choice.* The ideas of many people over many years have gone into making America what it is today, notes this artist, and that is the idea she wanted to express in this boldly designed quilt done in the colors of the flag. The stylized face, with ideas shooting like stars from the top of the head, represents the spirit of all the thinkers who contributed their work, creations, and thoughts to this country over the last five centuries (starting, the artist says, with Columbus and his new idea). Inge Schulz-Loeffler says that the stars on the crown of the Statue of Liberty inspired her dramatic use of stars in this quilt; not only do they symbolize America, but "they also symbolize new beginnings and new ideas." She had had the idea for the quilt for nearly a year but did not start working on it until two months before the deadline. Then, she laughs, "I went to my room to work and no one saw me for a long time!" It was difficult, she recalls, to translate the idea into fabric; the face especially, with its long thin lines that demanded regularity and precision, presented many technical difficulties in its execution, solved only by doing a lot of basting before she could actually begin to appliqué. She notes that once she starts on a quilt project, she prefers to work on it until it is done; to her, this also symbolizes what she believes is an American trait—"you start and you work until you have carried out an idea"—and it is an idea that she hopes is reflected in her quilt. The artist, who teaches retarded children when she is not quilting, was a country winner in the Memories of Childhood contest and has participated in many exhibits and contests in Europe, including Heidelberg's Quilt Bienialle in 1984 and 1988. "I was very happy about the Memories of Childhood contest," she says, "so I felt that I had to enter this one, too." Inge Schulz-Loeffler, a self-taught quilter who has now been quilting for about ten years, is a member of the Patchwork Gilde of North Germany and of Swiss Patchwork.

◆

FRIENDS

SHARING

AMERICA

◆

Edith and Polly by the Variable Star Quilters, Souderton, Pennsylvania. 1990. Cotton, lace. *First Place Grand Prize Winner.* "We started with the idea of sharing," say Norma Grasse, a member of the Variable Star Quilters, in explaining how the design came to be. "We tried to come up with all the things that you share—food, conversation, friendship, and so on. We also wanted a nostalgic theme, a sort of timeless painting, somehow related to history, and perhaps just a little ambiguous." This prize-winning design captures it all; the setting is Anywhere, U.S.A.; there is a definite period feel to the two central figures (vintage fabrics were used in the dresses, apron, and lace collar), who are engaged in a time-honored exchange, yet the viewer can't tell who is doing the giving and who is receiving—and that is as it should be. "The group," says Norma Grasse, spokesperson for the Variable Star Quilters, "is a cross-section of ages and community. Members come from a twenty-mile radius and cover three counties." Twelve of the seventeen members of the group actually worked on the quilt (because it was in the summer, some members were away on vacation), but moral encouragement and support came from all. Three members were responsible for the two figures and the porch and background, five members worked on the vine border, one person did the quilting, and the others did whatever else was necessary. The group chose fabric together, cut out and ironed the pieces together, and placed the pieces together, but the small appliqué work was done at home. "We tried to think of problems in advance, but it is still amazing that the work went so smoothly," Grasse says. "We work well together!" The Variable Star Quilters, a chapter of the National Quilters Association, started in 1978 and have carried out many joint projects, from raffle quilts to *The Quiltie Ladies Scrapbook* to a recent project involving reproducing thirty quilts from and the reprinting of a 1941 W.P.A. manual on quilts. *The Variable Star Quilters:* Sallie Astheimer, Sandy Barford, Ann Bean, Ann Chess, Jody Clemens, Nancy Coyle, Jan Deitcher, June Garges, Barb Garrett, Susan Goelz, Norma Grasse, Melissa Horn, Bev Musselman, Nancy Roan, Bertha Rush, Mary Shelly, Eleanor Shubert.

Quilters' Dwellings by the Red Apple Quilters, Royal Oak, Michigan. 1990. Cotton, cotton blends, silk organza, eyelet, plastic, braid, lace. *Second Place Grand Prize Winner.* This quilt design was inspired by one piece of fabric, says Annamae Kelly, the guiding force for the Red Apple Quilters. When she and Sharon Falberg of Bloomfield Hills, Michigan, one of the other makers, saw the fabric that now forms the inner border, they agreed that it had to be in the quilt. "As soon as I saw it, I knew that the theme should be the homes of the quilters, enclosed within the 'picket fence,' which is what the fabric reminded us of," says Kelly, who did the design for the quilt. She tried to make the homes as true to life as possible. "I even included the lamp post, rosebush, and iron railings on my gray ranch house," she laughs. Falberg's house, the tall white one, is actually one she had lived in when in London, but she liked it enough to include it here. The third house was that of a quilter who originally was scheduled to quilt the entire piece but who pulled out when she found out that the quilt included some machine piecing and plastic remnants in the windows of the houses. "We were down to the wire when she pulled out," Annamae Kelly recalls, "and there wasn't time to piece another house." They found a last-minute rescuer, however—Sue Nickels of Ann Arbor, Michigan. "Sharon knew of Sue's work from the Ann Arbor Quilt Guild, and so we asked her to step in and be our third person. We only really got to know each other after the quilt was done!" The composition of the Red Apple Quilters is informal and varies from quilt to quilt as Annamae Kelly, whose studio gives the group its name, asks different quilters to join in, depending on what the project is. She has often taught the quilters their craft, as in the case of Sharon Falberg. Kelly, now seventy-five, was trained as a painter but, she says, "once I started working with fabric, that was it! I never get bored." Her art expertise is evident in the hand-dyed and painted fabrics included in the quilt; her proficiency with these techniques is also what initially led her into teaching.

Patchwork Panorama by the Sonomarin Irregulars, Sonoma, California. 1990. Cotton, cotton blends. *Honorable Mention.* "We call ourselves the Sonomarin Irregulars AKA the Potato Chip Gang! We started with four members, had six when the quilt was started, five when it was quilted, and now have seven members. We started in 1989 as a regional minigroup of the East Bay Heritage Quilters, and we are spread across two counties north of San Francisco. None of us really knew each other before, and working on this quilt has really brought us together!" The group's name resulted from combining the names of the two counties the quilters represent—Sonoma and Marin—and the quilt includes a logo block (lower interior right corner) that is symbolic of the abundant agricultural and scenic attributes of the counties. "The blocks around the edge of the quilt each represent one of the fifty states, as well as one for our logo and one for our names. Each of us did our own heads and bodies, and we worked on the United States (for *US*) together. We divided up the state blocks to do individually, often choosing states we had lived in or ones that had special meaning to us. We all shared in planning the quilt, and we combined our fabric stashes for the map and the background." The colors used in the map of the United States are intended to give a sense of the topography of the country, with soft yellows for the rolling prairies of the heartland, greens for the verdant east and northwest, cool violets and purples for mountains, and earth tones for more arid areas. States are identified by cross-stitch abbreviations, and block patterns are a combination of traditional and original designs—the quilter's choice. This was the first project that the group had worked on as a whole and, although much was done individually, the women met at least monthly and once for three days at a mountain cabin in the Sierras in order to work together on the quilt. They note, "We are thrilled with the way it turned out!" *The Sonomarin Irregulars:* Janet Baldwin, Alice Friesen, Karen Mansergh, Nancy Parmelee, Elizabeth Secker.

Friends Sharing America by Three Friends, Clinton, Michigan. 1990. Cotton, cotton blends. Jacalyn Findley, Jane Handy, and Peg Voll are the Three Friends that make up the group that created this appealing quilt with an old-fashioned flair. This is the first project that they have worked on as a group, and they started because, they say, they "thought it would be fun to get together and do something like this. We all just love to quilt!" They note that the quilt was entirely created as a group, from the design through the stitching. "We wanted to capture a sense of the old generation and the new generation and the sharing of their different quilting techniques," they say of their stark outlined figures, reminiscent of the silhouette portraits of the early nineteenth century, which are shown working on a colorful quilt in the traditional Log Cabin pattern. The cuddly animal at the edge of the quilt is symbolic of all the cats and dogs that have proved quilters' friends through the ages! The deceptively simple design, carefully contrasted colors, and meticulous stitching all combine successfully to generate the impression of sharing through the ages that was their goal. They initially met twice a week, working as a whole on the quilt; later, when the piecing and appliqué were completed, they took turns taking the piece home for a week at a time to do some quilting, then they would get together and work jointly again. During the course of the quilt's construction, the Three Friends only had one problem: "None of us had ever used a marker to sketch our quilt lines before, and we decided to use one on this quilt. We had a really hard time getting the ink out!" The instructions with the marker recommended washing the fabric soon after the marker was used, and the Three Friends waited nearly a year before washing the quilt. "We really had to scrub hard to remove the ink," they now recall. Although the three women had a good time making the quilt, when Peg Voll, the motivator for this project, asked her friends whether they wanted to start another quilt, "they just laughed at me," she says, "and said 'Maybe next spring!'"

Threads of Friendship by the Cocheco Quilters Guild, Rochester, New Hampshire. 1990. Cotton, wool, lace, fur, ribbons, plastic charms. *Honorable Mention.* In this fanciful quilt, a map of the United States is divided into "quilt regions" instead of states. The map is surrounded by a personalized border of hands—hands that include favorite jewelry, carefully polished nails, and special attributes, such as a slate for a teacher—traced from those of the guild members, friends, and family; friendship sayings are written in between the hands. A "thread of friendship" connects all the hands together. "Even though the U.S.A. is big, we are all tied together with a common thread—our quilts," says Susan Bickford of the Cocheco Quilters Guild. "Many hands have made quilts to keep our families warm through the years!" This Guild started fifteen years ago with thirteen members; it now has 150, and the group together has carried out a number of communal projects, from making quilts for the homeless and for unwed mothers to creating raffle quilts for various causes. The incipient idea for this quilt originated with member Faye Labanaris (a winner in both the Memories of Childhood and Discover America contests), was brainstormed into reality by a group of twelve, and eventually involved eighteen members in its creation. Map sections and hands were done individually; sections were sewn together and the map and hands positioned and appliquéd at meetings of all those involved in the project. At one point, there was concern that all the hands made the quilt too busy, but an emergency meeting brought all the "lovers of hands" out, and so the design remained. Faye Labanaris also kept a running journal of progress on the quilt; an excerpt from the meeting where all pieces were put together for the first time for all members to see: "Opinion was unanimous—it's wonderful!" *The Cocheco Quilters:* Jan Abbott, Ginny Adams, Dee Angelopoulos, Maggie Beal, Judith Berlo-Tucker, Susan Bickford, Joan Considine, Lyn DiGregorio, Patience Dixon, Susan Fell, Louise Ford, Peggy Frangos, Michelle Kincaid, Faye Labanaris, Wen Redmond, Barbara Russell, Susan Savory, Linda Sherf, Linda Sherman.

And Crown Thy Good with Brotherhood by the Delectable Mountain Quilters, South Royalton, Vermont. 1990. Cotton, corduroy, metallic fabrics. Since this charming quilt was first started, Marge Morrison, a lively eighty-two-year-old quilter who conceived its design and drew the patterns for the quilters to follow, has lost her eyesight. The quilt was completed and entered in this contest in large part as a labor of love and as a token of the affection and high regard that the other quilters comprising the Delectable Mountain Quilters feel for this outstanding member who is now retired and lives part-time in Florida. The quilt depicts a nostalgic look at many aspects of American life from its beginning to the present, at work and at play, East and West, North and South. Barnraising, square dancing, jazz, golf, maple sugaring, travel by covered wagon, skiing, bathing, skating, and picnics in the park are among the many activities, sites, and events shown—and, of course, quilting has a prominent place! The quilt is framed by a stitched border of outlined paper doll-like figures that hold hearts instead of hands and "signifies the brotherhood of mankind" to this group of quilters. The Delectable Mountain Quilters was started about nine years ago by a few women who thought a group would provide quilting stimulus as well as a good reason to socialize! They canvased ten or twelve towns within their county and now have a membership of twenty-eight, sixteen of whom worked on this quilt. It is a diversified group, running the age range from thirty-six to eighty-two, with quilting skills just as varied—from beginners to experts. Many in the group met for the first time through their meetings and many good friendships have developed as a result. The Delectable Mountain Quilters have worked on over twenty quilts together, including a fundraiser quilt, for which everyone made a block, for the Quilt Museum in Lowell, Massachusetts. *Delectable Mountain Quilters:* Edith Artz, Mary Ellen Benson, Nellie Burmaster, Charlotte Croft, Ruth Delaney, Betty Fretz, Shirley Garafano, Cyndy Gates, Meg Jillson, Deborah King, Polly Leavitt, Loeky Merlo, Marge Morrison, Marge Rafuse, Sue Schoolcraft, Corinne Stewart.

Sharing America by the Little Stitch Makers, La Crosse, Wisconsin. 1990. Cotton. "Sharing" is the key word for this quilt, and for the three women who made it—Louise Zoerb, Sharon Slimmen, and Marilyn Conway. They shared their labor, their vision of America (they believe sharing is what made this country great), and even the name of their group—Little Stitch Makers—in which the initial letter of each word stands for the first name of each of "the quilters." Louise Zoerb had the inspiration to enter the contest and "hand-picked" the other quilters, who were old friends; they had all been members of the La Crosse Area Quilters. She spent three months creating the design, a Wisconsin farm scene that included three generations of quilters working on a quilt, surrounded by an inner border of traditional quilt blocks representing both geographic regions and cross-country interests. The four corner blocks—an American eagle, the Liberty Bell, the flag, and the torch of the Statue of Liberty—are the symbols of American freedom. The outer border, quilted in a wave pattern, represents the oceans surrounding the country, and a tribute to Columbus's voyage is shown in one corner. Louise Zoerb, a medical technologist, found designing the quilt to be a daunting task; her previous quilts had all been traditional patterns and she had no artistic training, but her friends gave her the support needed to do the job. The three quilters chose the fabric together in an Amish quilt shop in Iowa, making joint decisions on color and balance. Louise Zoerb made the central scene (the miniature quilt on which the quilters are working contains a scrap of every fabric used in the quilt), and all three worked on the surrounding blocks. Together they cut out the pieces, then worked on their individual blocks at home. The Little Stitch Makers often joked that their chances of being included among the winners was "like a needle in a haystack," thus leading Louise Zoerb to add a haystack to the quilt! The success of this quilt, as well as the "wonderful time" that they had during its production, has resulted in the group's decision to continue working together making other quilts and to enter more contests.

Postage Stamp Quilt by the Mavericks, with quilters from four countries and ten states. 1990. Cotton. In a widespread cooperative effort that covered a major portion of the world, the *Postage Stamp Quilt*, a double-sided work, was conceived and created by focusing on one pattern of friendship—communication by mail. One side of the quilt is a composite of fabric envelopes from the twenty-six people, ranging in age from fifteen to sixty-five, who helped to make it; the flip side, designed by Robin Lambie Smith, the motivator for this extraordinary effort, represents a single postage stamp, an abstract amalgam of brilliant color. Many of the quilters have never met except through their long-distance participation in this project; each created an envelope with a real or imaginary stamp on it, then sent it to Robin Smith who, with the help of Kathleen Francis, laid out the envelopes into a pleasing collage and pieced the quilt together. All submissions were used, including the unfinished envelope by Robin Smith's fifteen-year-old daughter, Julia, who had only gotten as far as her return address by the deadline. Her mother marked it *Returned for Postage* and incorporated it, too! Robin Smith's idea with this massive undertaking was to express her belief that quilting has always been a way for women to speak to other women, that it is a shared experience. "This quilt is in keeping with the idea of the friendship quilt and that what people contributed on different levels was valuable," she notes. "The quilt was definitely a positive experience—and mostly due to the involvement of other people!" *The Mavericks:* **Australia**—Narelle Grieve; **Japan**—Hitomi Kurosowa; **Sweden**—Christina Kellström; **United States**—*California:* Sue Handley Poteat; *Connecticut:* Linda Jesse; *Delaware:* Nancy Stanford Davis; *Maryland:* Jeanne Benson, Joan Siegal; *Massachusetts:* Gail Binney-Stiles, Vickie Wilder; *Michigan:* Molly Sieg; *New York:* Linda Reinagel; *Pennsylvania:* Marcia Baehr, Gail Donkin, Kathleen Wixted Francis (quilter), Sue Frazier, Karen Giuliano, Marilyn Grant, Betty Plummer, Gloria Polen, Nancy Rose, Julia Smith, Robin Lambie Smith, Margaret Van Gilder; *Texas:* Jane Sowell; *Washington:* Lorrie Sjoquist.

59

Boreal Meadow by the Group of Five, Niagara Penninsula, Ontario, Canada. 1990. Silk, cotton, cotton blends, metallic fabrics and threads. *Honorable Mention*. The brilliance of an Arctic sky provides a striking contrast to glowing crystalline shapes that capture the eye and the imagination in this stunning abstract design. The five-sided figures are representational both of the gorgeous snowflake-like blossoms found in a boreal meadow at its springtime prime and of the five women who created this colorful fantasy. Also, the artists note, the figure allows for a freedom of shape and form that lends itself well to the impressionistic image they wished to give in this elegant vision that seems to float and shimmer within the quilt's boundaries. The design was conceived of by the group as a whole, and they spent about six weeks refining their idea until they felt that the reality of the design could match what they had imagined. The choice of fabrics and threads was also a crucial element in the final visual impact that the quilt would have, as they wanted to share with the viewer the "vibrancy and intensity that is found in the Arctic blooms" for so short a period of the year. The Group of Five represent a range of backgrounds and talents, from business to nursing to art, but all are united by their love of and skill in quilting. They spent approximately a day a week working together on this project; they also "did their homework" when the project required it! The quilters say that although the theme was appealing, entering an international competition was a challenge in itself; the project also allowed them the opportunity to expand their own knowledge of their art as well as stimulate new ideas for the future. Marilyn Walker, one member of the Group and a fifteen-year quilting veteran, notes that the work in this quilt "was among the most complex sewing that I have ever seen. All the intersections (and there are many) are so beautifully matched! I believe that this quilt could not have been executed by any one of us on our own." *The Group of Five:* Irja Donoghue, Mary Filek, Marion Hardy, Cheryl Schonewille, Marilyn Walker.